Tell It As It Is!

The Sequel

By Charles Parker

ANOTHER NO HOLDS BARRED

Story of a Family Living

With Severe Autism

Published in 2023 by Charles Parker

ISBN 978-1-7393478-9-5

www.tellitasitis.uk

Tell It As It Is - htttps://www.facebook.com/groups/111759617555183

Design by Interpro Publishing Solutions

Table of Contents

DEDICATION

It's well worth a read and is dedicated to my son Christopher, all of my supportive family and those affected by ASD across the World.

When I wrote my first book, Tell It As It Is, I was lucky enough to have one of our customers, a lady named Phillis Painter, who was a retired teacher that took on the task of proof reading the book.

Phillis said about the book that it may move you to tears and will certainly give readers a clearer insight into the trials, tribulations and amazingly sometimes joy of being a parent in this family.

If I am honest, I must say that I truly believe that this, my second book, Tell It As It Is – The Sequel continues where the first book left off, full of trials and tribulations that we have had to endure. It has been Tina's and my mission to showcase autism as it really is and to show how as parents, we have navigated the highs and the lows of bringing up a child with extremely complex needs.

Many, if they were writing this story, may have wanted to cover up some of the truth, but not me. The idea is for every reader to know the truth, to feel the difficulties Tina and I have had to endure. To understand how traumatic, it can become when you are advocating for your child.

As you read this story you will I hope have a smile now and then, just like we have at some of Christopher's antics.

I guess the most important thing, and a message to everyone in similar circumstances, is that at no time did we think of giving up. As things got really bad for Chris at the residential home, we had only one thing on our mind.

TO WIN THE DAY – TO GET HIM OUT OF THERE AND BRING HIM BACK NEARER TO OUR HOME.

NOW'S THE TIME FOR YOU TO FIND OUT IF WE SUCCEEDED.

A Tribute for my dear old Dad for telling my story.

ACKNOWLEDGEMENTS

To Kate Landells, head teacher at Hill House School and her amazing team who collectively made such a difference to our son. Kate placed her arms around us as a family, realised we needed help and did everything to ensure it was delivered.

To Clare Sines, NHS Commissioner / Case Manager. The lady that stepped up and made sure Chris was kept safe after he had been abused and neglected at his residential care home. Clare never just talked the talk, she got on and took action, working tirelessly for Chris and for us. Clare left a legacy for us to continue her mission, for a young man she clearly cared for so much. We were devastated when she left and was replaced.

To Thornbury Nursing, those wonderful band of nurses, second to none, who stepped in at the drop of a hat in 2015 and again at the latter end of 2021 for almost two years. You are all so amazing and we are so grateful.

To Sophie Pinder and her management team at Kind Tailored Care that recognised Chris was someone special, that he needed special care, that we as parents were fighting his cause and despite knowing she would have to deliver specialist care for far less than her normal rates.

To Fran Lloyd, Senior Occupational Therapist. Whilst Fran wanted to help our son she was continually lied to and hindered when she enquired after Christopher. Many would have given up, but not Fran. As soon as she heard Chris did need help, she stepped straight in spending many hours with him, discovering and providing what he needed. We feel sorry for this very knowledgeable lady whose professional advice was not listened to by the ICB or local authority, ultimately affecting the care that our son requires.

To my dear friend Colin Osborne, who, as a professional photographer and without any delay agreed to take and edit the pictures that we needed for the book, including the front cover.

Finally, I want to thank my dear wife Tina for her help with this book and for the lifetime of dedication and love she has shown for Christopher. She has spent many an hour brainstorming with me to ensure that as much as possible of the stand out moments in Christopher's life have been recorded. She wrote a chapter of her own and the most beautiful poem written on Christopher's behalf.

Thank you, Tina.

If I have missed anyone out that I should have acknowledged and thanked, I apologise from the bottom of my heart.

INTRODUCTION

Hi and a Big Hello again to the many that read my first book that was published all the way back in 2007. A very warm welcome to those that have not yet discovered "Tell It As It Is" and just to let you know that is still available.

It's been over 15 years since I put pen to paper and exposed the world to what it was like living each and every day of our lives with a severely autistic child. It was a NO HOLDS BARRED true story designed to help the many parents that found themselves in the same boat without a clue what to expect and where to look for help.

No holds barred and written from the heart. I am not a scientist and therefore not able to have any clinical input. I just wanted to help others understand how we dealt with so many different situations.

From many of the fantastic reviews I received, readers said it was the honesty that made it an irresistible read and an enormous help to them. When autism knocks on your door it can bring with it stress that attacks many a partnership or marriage. Maybe you already know this but for those that don't here's a fact that can make bringing up a child with autism so very difficult.

Eighty percent, yes, I did say 80% of Partnerships or marriages that involve autism, break down and what makes it even worse is that it's nearly always the male partner that walks away, leaving a mum on her own, perhaps struggling to make ends meet.

The idea of bringing our true story to as many that have the time to read and more importantly to those that need some support is paramount. The way I write this second book or sequel if you wish will not differ from the first.

Please or offend, that's me, I'm afraid. I will continue to tell my readers exactly how the struggles with authorities have panned out. More importantly is that I let you all know of the love and joy that Christopher has brought to our lives.

We have had many battles during Christopher's life to ensure his quality of life does not decline and on the contrary improves at every possible opportunity.

Some of the most difficult things to deal with or overcome have been when social workers or those in authority believe they have the right to dictate to you how your child should be brought up and where they should be brought up often related to the budget, they say is available. Sometimes through our son's twenty-four years we have been blessed with amazing people that wanted to work with us to ensure the best outcomes. Then there are those that consider they have the God dammed right to take over. To make it as difficult as they can for you, to find faults that do not exist and to think that they are better than you are, that over the twenty-four years that you have worked to enhance your child's life, in their opinion, you have fallen woefully short.

I am convinced that had we not become Legal Deputies to Christopher one person in particular, would have done their best to walk all over us. The person I am referring to is a case manager. During their period in that position, they have formed all of their opinions from paperwork and quite likely hearsay. Not once, up to the time I am writing this introduction, have they taken to the road and visited Christopher, to build a relationship with our young man and be able to make honest assessments of his situation and help him.

One thing that both my wife Tina and I have is courage to take these people on and to ensure they never get the chance to throw their weight around and to influence the years ahead.

There are many wonderful stories to read in the pages ahead, as well as those that have definitely not been so good. Please, take time to read, to enjoy and to learn from our journey.

I hope and indeed pray that every page you read will bring you something very special. Enjoy. Charles.

PREFACE

Many, I know, will have read my first book and will have learnt what it was like for us as parents in Christophers early years. However, what I perhaps didn't tell you enough about was how, when finding out Chris had severe autism, that had such a profound effect upon us both and how we dealt with those early years.

I was invited to speak to an audience of nurses' doctors and other professionals back in 2006 and that talk has not been aired since then. To give you an incite of Christopher's early years I have decided to dust it off and include it right here, so you can read for yourself more of the journey we have been on.

Once you have read the following called Heaven and Hell I do hope you will enjoy and learn from this, my second book.

HEAVEN OR HELL

Does Anyone know what it's like to be in heaven and then suddenly find, in the gasp of breath, or the snap of your fingers you have reached hell. That's exactly what it felt like for my wife Tina and me when we were told that our youngest son was probably autistic, it felt like someone had torn our hearts out and left us in a total void.

Somehow, we both found the strength to come to terms with this, then, suddenly there it was again, "HELL". Our older son was also diagnosed with a problem. How could it be, both boys had been so normal when they were born and in their early years.

Let me set the scene and explain just how our lives have unfolded. Before I do however, I want to make it quite clear to anyone who like us, reaches those gates of hell, that it is not all doom and gloom. I want to tell it as it was for us but assure you all that out of our adversity there has come just as much happiness.

So where did it all start? Tina and I had been happily married with two young sons, Charlie the oldest by 18 months and Christopher. I was running a successful driving school; Tina working her homebased business part time. It seemed everything was in place for a bright future. Then came the first bombshell! At about 14 months old Christopher seemed to stop eye contact and appeared not to hear us when we spoke to him. Up until then he had been a perfectly normal little boy. After talking to the GP and a referral to the Pediatrician a hearing test was arranged at the hospital. Chris seemed to fool us all for a while but then passed a more intensive hearing test, so we were back to square one.

After more consultation it was decided to refer Chris to Wordsworth house and after 10 weeks, aged 2 years nine months, he was diagnosed with severe Autism and developmental delay. Severe autism, that's not so bad we thought; if it gets no worse than this we can cope as he came across as a quiet little soul. Little did we know. Weeks and months went by and Chris developed all sorts of habits, some dangerous, some totally unexplainable. These ranged from twisting string round fingers, biting both himself and others, head banging and breaking windows, posting, screaming, tearing anything up including his clothes to name but a few. We were heartbroken; our lives were turned upside down.

Fortunately, we were pointed to the direction of a project called "SCAMP". This was a project run by Southampton University to prove to the government that ABA (Applied Behavior Analysis) would be an advantage to all autistic children. Chris in fact was the first child on this project and it involved 6 hours a day, seven days a week, very intensive work within our home. Christopher responded well and some of his speech returned but the intensity both on him and us as parents took its toll and after 18 months, we called time.

By now the autism had really started to kick in and at that point he was not on any medication. He had started smearing in his bedroom and peeling the paint and plaster off of his walls. Very few nights went by where one or both of us were not up most of the night to stop him selfharming. Many's the night where we thought he had settled down; we would just get settled and he would start up again. In we would go only to find him and the walls covered in faeces. One would clean the room the other clean Chris up and hope he didn't perform again that night. The only way we found to calm him down some nights was for me to take him out in the car and drive round, sometimes for over two hours, and then carefully, oh so carefully, lift him back to his room. Tina and I are not ashamed to admit that many times we have found ourselves crying and wondering where it was all going to end.

End, it never will of course but time has taught us that you can come to terms with it all to a certain degree. Chris continued to be difficult, breaking up so many things in the home, causing us all sorts of problems when we took him out none more so than the embarrassment of having people look at us as if we were all weird. Eventually Christopher was put on Ritalin and this seemed to have a bit of a calming influence although now when he is on 60mgs daily sometimes you do wonder if it is doing any good. Could it be that these kids get addicted? At present he is at Ridgeway House School and he proves to be a right handful for them some days. I believe it fair to say he is probably the most difficult child in the school at present and without doubt according to his pediatrician the worst case of autism in a child that she has come across in the whole of her career. We have more than one reason that has persuaded us to apply for a place at Hope Lodge.

For all of the trials he has caused us, even bringing the lounge ceiling down by flooding the upstairs, he is such a lovable boy. Other claims to fame include breaking my shoulder whilst I was driving. Yes! It's true. He is in a special harness and has to sit in the centre of the back row of seats, of my vehicle I use for driving instruction. as any others would allow him to head butt the windows, the problem being when he has a "Paddy" he kicks out at me. I was lucky enough to be provided with protective shields, at a cost of £700. You know the type, the ones the police and taxi drivers have to protect them. Well, if you haven't guessed by now I can tell you, he's broken them and they are being sent back. It's back to the drawing board.

Now, before I get too engrossed in more of Christopher's antics let me tell you a little about Charlie. "Back To Hell". Yes, we had all the heartache of finding out about Chris to relive when Charlie was about four years six months. He started by fooling his teacher. Making out he did not understand and getting one to one special help; something that was found to be not needed right at that time. He was so clever at leading them up the garden path. At Home he was looking for any reason to get special attention, was it jealousy perhaps.

He would climb on top of the tall furniture to enable him to write on the ceiling and then one night he came downstairs and said, "Daddy my light's not working". No wonder: when I went in his room I had a shock, he had used the top bunk to jump off, used the light cord as a Tarzan rope and pulled the ceiling down.

At school he started hiding under desks and refused totally to come out when told. Charlie was diagnosed with Emotional and Behavioral disorder.

To this day we are not sure if the correct diagnosis was made and we are in the process of having more investigations made. It is possible he could have Aspergers.

Whatever, Tina and I just carry on. Do we get weary? Yes of course we do but like any good parents you just take things in your stride. There is one thing you all have to remember and that is if you want something shout long and loud. It's not very often that someone will come along and say would you like this benefit or how can we help you in the home. As parents Tina and I have fought tooth and nail for everything we have. Both boys have special bedrooms now, Charlie's more by accident as the one he has was destined for Christopher but it wasn't suitable. Someone had signed for it so it couldn't go back.

Chris now has a fully padded bedroom, believed to be perhaps the only one in the area, where he can sleep and play safely. Of course, he still smears but believe me it is far easier to wipe those walls clean than it was before.

I suppose the biggest change in the home is the smell, it was awful. But now with no carpet in Chris's room and no plaster for things to seep into life is somewhat more pleasant. Glass throughout the home has been changed to toughened, the sun lounge has been fitted inside and out with bomb proof film and every door in the house has a lock on it to contain both the little beauties, so they remain in our sight at most times.

The latest addition was an air conditioning unit to control the temperature in Christopher's room. No one realized it would reach over 100 degrees Fahrenheit during the summer. What I am saying is help is out there; don't be afraid to ask for it. If someone says no first time round keep asking until you get what you want.

A bold decision was made at the start of 2004 to give up my driving school and to work Tina's business full time whilst the children are at school. This has allowed me to be on hand to help with the children in the evenings and at weekends. Our major goal this year is to work hard to enable us to buy a Motor Home or seven-seater vehicle. This will allow us to sit Chris further back, hence not being able to kick me, or pull his mum's hair but more importantly have the opportunity to take some breaks as a family.

We cannot do this at present for fear of what the boys might do, proof being when we took Charlie away for a weekend last year whilst Chris was in respite and he decided to wet the bed in the caravan on both nights. How embarrassing was that?

I could seriously write a book; maybe one day I will, there is so much to tell but would like to conclude now by telling you how we seem to cope with the challenges we have faced and how we will continue to face those in the future.

You know life is all about choices. We all have a choice. Tina and I could have chosen to lie down and surrender to the challenges and problems that have confronted us. We made a choice; We chose not to lie down but to face up to the challenges, to fight for what we want, for what we feel is best for our boys.

When you make your choice, please remember you need not be alone, look for help, it's out there. It would be so easy for anyone in our position to constantly portray ourselves as sad persons but here is a great tip on how to start each and every day, one that we do without fail.

When you get out of bed every morning, look in the mirror and smile. You know what! You'll always get a smile back. Best wishes to all.

Charles

Charles Parker

CHAPTER 1

Where Were We?

I suppose one of the most difficult things you need to do when you continue a true story is to make sure, especially after 15 years, that you carry on from where you left off, without missing anything significant.

Well, if my memory serves me right, Tell It As It Is, finished at the time Christopher was doing well, having settled into a local specialist autistic school. It was, at the time, so lovely to think that we had finally found somewhere that Chris appeared to be happy and had started to settle into a great routine.

Mind, we did have to have one very early battle, using some tricks we had up our sleeves, to secure the placement. The male social worker at the time was also a tree surgeon and repeatedly told us, "You won't get your son in there". After numerous meetings and a panel review where we tipped out a massive bag of clothes Chris had been allowed to tear up at his first school, shocking the panel members, we won the day and you can probably guess that my advice to the guy with his negative attitude was that maybe he should stick to his pruning. In fact, that may well have been what happened as he was not around for too much longer. We had to move on to another social worker, in the hope that we may have someone better.

How strange though, that a time of happiness can change in an instant. What caused the sudden change, the demise in our son and why did his behaviours change for the worse.

I suppose a simple answer that came to mind was all there in one word. "Change". Some of you may know and understand that one of the worst things that can happen to an autistic child is change. They do not appreciate change! Even to take a different route on a regular journey could send Christopher rocking.

We are only at the very start of the ongoing journey for my son but as we make our way through his school years you will realise there is a common factor that will explain so much.

In any normal school children generally make progress by starting in Reception, then year one right the way through to year 11 and sometimes beyond, changing classes and teachers each year of the journey.

With special needs, it's all so different. A disabled child may find themselves staying in a class, with the same teacher for at least a couple of years, sometimes longer. That can have fantastic results and for sure it helped Christopher, until he was hit with major changes.

His first two years at this specialist school for autistic children went so well. Many of his behaviours improved as did some of his academics, in particular learning to write for the very first time. Christopher had learnt to trust his teacher and the three classroom assistants, who were always on hand to help him through difficult times. Barbara, being the lead in the class, then two ladies named Carol. For the life of me I cannot remember the name of the third assistant, but they were all absolutely brilliant.

Certainly, one of the most memorable times I can remember in Chris's early days at this school was receiving a phone call from his teacher insisting we put everything on the back burner and get into school to see what our son had achieved. We wasted no time, into the car, off to the school and were greeted by a jubilant Barbara. What was it that she knew, and we were about to discover? We were taken into the classroom and directed to one particular wall on which the word HOME had been written. Christopher's first written communication. Of course, what wasn't immediately obvious to us but struck us a little later that day was that it also meant our son had learnt to spell and of course to some extent read.

Home, why had he chosen to write this particular word? To this day neither my wife Tina nor I can really say we understand but WOW what a wonderful surprise, our son, starting to write. It was without doubt a momentous moment for us both and one we shall never forget.

It meant something to Chris for sure, but we, like those fantastic ladies that cared for our son, day in and day out could not work it out.

What was noticeable at this time was the improvement in behaviours, the ripping of clothes had decreased, and it was so obvious Chris had grown to trust those that spent so much of their time with him.

Even at the Lodge, where Chris slept through the weekdays there were signs of a different young lad developing. We visited the Lodge every Wednesday evening, and it was a pleasure to see our son relaxing and playing in the playground, generally having fun which is what every young child should be doing.

One of his tricks at the Lodge was Posting or hiding anything that could be pushed behind furniture, leaving everyone wondering what had happened to this, where had that gone? Much of this happened when inside and did not become evident until you went outside. For he had the habit of stuffing things behind the soft furnishings that protected many of the windows. There they were, in full view once you were outside looking in but most of his hidden treasures were impossible to retrieve as they were well and truly stuffed away.

It was interesting to see his face when he realised what we were looking at. Sometimes, a favourite old phrase was used by Chris, one he often used when he had been up to mischief. "What have you Done? He would say it with that cheeky grin on his sweet little innocent face. Once he said this, no matter what the occasion you knew you were looking for something, that he had either hidden, broken or destroyed, or had something planned for that particular toy or game and it was then a competition, whether you were able to rescue the object, or he was too quick for you.

Chris would look, when outside, at some of the mysteries he had produced, and one could almost see a wry smile enter his beautiful yet innocent face. I can imagine, in his mind, that he might have thought, Christopher did that. Two words that he might have used, had he watched the comedy series on television, "Miranda", may have been, "Such Fun"!

Of course, whilst we and the staff may have been annoyed on the inside, you just could not help seeing the funny side of so many of his antics.

You know I cannot remember if I told you in my first book about a very amusing music lesson. Never mind if I have, it's so funny and worth hearing again. Do you remember the two guys advertising 118 118? Well, on this lovely afternoon, the children were gathered for assembly and were to be introduced to their new deputy head teacher. I can't remember who introduced her to the class, but it went something like this. "Ok children, just a bit of hush please, I'd like to introduce you to Maureen now, the new deputy head. Without any hesitation, with the school hall absolutely in silence, a rare occasion of course, Christopher stood up and recited at the top of his voice, "Oh Maureen, She's cheap". Apparently, there was not a dry eye in the room.

Comedy entertainment at a top level without having to book it or pay for it.

Chris could however be so different, particularly towards his brother Charlie, just 18 months older but very fearful of Christopher when he came home at weekends. There was no doubting about who was the boss. Had Chris had a dictionary of his own the word Fear would not have been included.

Even back at Ridgeway House where pupils ranged from 5 to 18, Christopher thought he has in charge. A bouncy castle had been provided and this 18-year-old Downs lad was enjoying his turn on the castle. His turn had lasted too long as far as Chris was concerned and he was on that castle in seconds, laying in to the 18-year-old and pushing him off. Chris was jubilant and the 18 year old, shocked I think, and he certainly did not go on the bouncy castle again, nor did he go near Christopher again that day.

So, there the scene is set, you now understand how difficult it was for Charlie, perhaps difficult just to understand why his brother enjoyed laying into him. It was so important that as parents we had to do something special for Charlie, to give him our uninterrupted time free from his brother and to be able to have fun. That had much to do with our decision for Chris to go into residential care during the week and just coming home at weekends.

At the time we had saved up enough money to think about a decent holiday. Now, where had Charlie mentioned, every time he saw the place on the telly. Why, every kids dream, Florida. Excited, I was ecstatic as I knew from taking my older children to Florida in 1993, what a fantastic time awaited Charlie and indeed his mum because she had not been to America either.

I could not wait to break the news. As soon as I did there was like a great big deep hole that had opened up and I had fallen right in. What was wrong, it was a great idea, what an amazing opportunity to spend that all so precious time with our son that put up with so much from his brother. It was indeed my wife, Charlie's mum, that added the damper to the plans.

"How can we go if we don't have anyone to look after Chris at the weekends". She continued, "It's ok through Monday to Friday for those two weeks, Chris is at school, but we have no one to look after him at the weekends."

"Don't worry", I said, we'll contact the people that offer support sometimes when Chris is at home. Sure enough, they were confident they could help and gave us a quote. From three in the afternoon through to nine on a Monday morning, for two weekends the quote was well in excess of four thousand pounds. A quote that to be honest would have put the holiday beyond us.

Worse was to come when they invited Christopher to visit the home for a day. Some day that was! It only lasted just a few hours, we received a phone call and a message saying sorry that's not for us. Here we were, holiday already booked and we're not able to go.

Now, I am well known for giving up on nothing. There has to be a way. We need to look at this problem, excuse me referring to my son as a problem, I don't mean it that way, but it boiled down to the same thing. Having asked the school if they could keep Chris over for a couple of weekends and being told that was impossible, I started to drop hints to those that I thought might be in need of some extra cash. Bingo! Looking for someone to look after Little Chris. It was Big Chris that came to our rescue, bless him. He and his partner offered to stay in our bungalow at the weekends we were away, whilst Chris would remain in school during the weekdays. It was a fabulous arrangement. Our Chris knew Big Chris well from school. Big Chris and his loved one pocketed a decent amount to help with their finances and we were able to take Charlie to Florida for his first break in years since the disaster spent in Grand Canaria when Christopher was just a very young lad, that constantly screamed and almost got us deported. God only knows, how we managed to stay in that hotel was a miracle. Probably the only thing on our side was the fact we owned a Time Share at that very hotel.

Nevertheless, Charlie had what he deserved, the holiday of a lifetime in Florida. A ten-berth bungalow so he could choose a different bed every night if he wished and his own private swimming pool that backed on to a wild nature reserve. Right up his street. Disney, was of course, the icing on the cake.

We saw a different Charlie whilst on that holiday, no signs of worry or anxiety, it was such a pleasure and we shall be forever grateful to good old Big Chris for the very important part he played in the lives of two brothers.

Whilst Christopher continued in Class 1 and appeared to be doing so well a visit to the eye hospital confirmed he had a very bad squint in both eyes and that they needed urgent attention. If his eyes were not sorted soon, they could be a problem for the rest of his life. What we did discover at that time is that our son had eyesight in line with that of a fighter pilot. Amazing, but without an operation soon his sight could be badly affected.

We knew Chris would not take kindly to anaesthetic, but it had to be arranged. It was just a matter of weeks and Chris was called in to Southampton Eye hospital, known to be one of the best in the world, we had every confidence in the surgeon that would perform what proved to be, to us a miracle.

Yes, Christopher was difficult when he came round from his operation, like a raging bull, with almost as much strength but the most important thing was that the surgery had been successful and had only enhanced the beauty that our little boy already possessed. What helped to calm Chris was simply a bit of wisdom from us, mum and dad. When Chris had a previous operation to have nine teeth extracted, we calmed him as soon as he came round with two, perhaps three readymade jellies. Just as the last time the jellies came to our rescue. Most importantly was that the nurses and the surgeon listened to us before the eye operation and the jellies were at the ready.

One of the trips out with the school that we really enjoyed was to Marwell Zoo, just a short journey, 30 minutes or so from where we lived. Whenever one of the excursions was organised by the Daily Echo and the management at Marwell, the whole complex was closed for the evening to the general public allowing only disabled children and their carers access. It was just amazing.

To keep Christopher under control we had him in his buggy, where he felt safe. Chris mainly enjoyed seeing lots of the staff from the zoo dressed up and entertaining whoever they could. I remember one guy being dressed as a monkey and popping in and out of the bushes. He had Christopher in fits of giggles, so much so that our happy little boy kept saying more. We took turns to push Chris around whilst the other enjoyed looking at the real animals and chatting to Charlie, whose interest was so great in animal life having already read so many Readers Digest books even at his young age. He would even contradict adults on many animal discussions, full of confidence that he was right.

I must tell you, something that really surprised us was the fact that Christopher's favourite animals were the giraffes, so tall and mighty and yet he showed no fear of them at all when he entered their inner enclosure. Whenever he has returned to Marwell he has always made sure he revisits his friends with the very long legs and long necks.

As each academic year at any school draws to an end it is usual to have some sort of sports day and this school was no exception. I always remember the first one at this school, lots of fun, lots of great food that Chris and the other kids loved. I suppose, though, the standout moments were seeing Chris inside a sack, jumping up and down and eventually falling over the line and when he joined his mum in a race around the perimeter of the sports field. I haven't got a clue who won, no one cared really, it was the joy for all the parents to see the interaction of the children, prepared to have a go at anything.

You may be wondering why I didn't take part. Let's make my excuse now and hope you'll all accept it. Just 12 weeks before sports day that year I had a knee replacement operation and it was not behaving too well. In fact it's never behaved very well and I have been in immense chronic pain still to this day. Even after a second opinion I was told, "Nothing we can do now, learn to live with it." So, I have done just that, got on with my life determined to still do whatever I can do to help my family, to have fun and to ensure both of the boys have plenty of whatever it is that they want.

I must remember this book, like my first, is supposed to tell you about our life and struggles with autism, not about myself. I can assure there is so much more to come, we have only just started, although we are just about to pass through what might be thought the saddest period in Christopher's time at this autism specific establishment. Yes, two years completed and the first major change, the first struggle for Chris as he is forced to change classes.

Barbara, his class teacher for so long had decided to retire along with one of the other support teachers, whilst the other two were going to be moved into new classes, with different pupils. If I am honest, I don't think anyone was happy, not even the two that were saying goodbye to the school for ever. Oh Barbara, why did you have to go?

Age 2¹ᐟ²

Top: *Taken in Hyde Park, Londc*

Middle & Bottom: *At home around the time of diagnosis.*

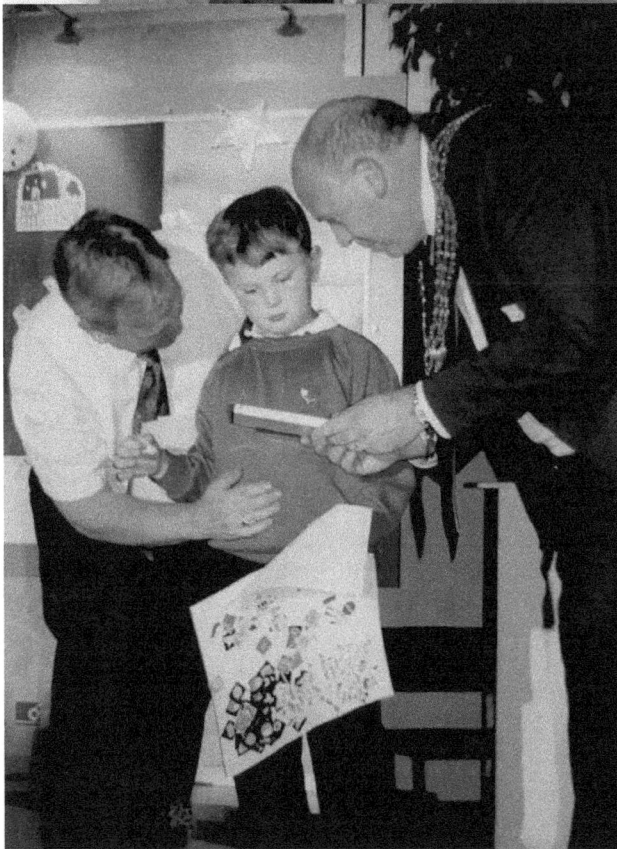

Aged 7-8

Left: *Chris recieving an award for the Child with Special Needs to make the most progress right across Hampshire.*

Charles Parker

CHAPTER 2

Chalk and Cheese

This next part of my story goes backwards before moving forward, I'm sure you'll understand once you have taken in this whole chapter.

You see Christopher does and quite rightly so have a mind of his own. After the first year with Barbara the idea was to move Chris into class 2, but he was having none of it. Yes, he was moved but he was definitely not happy. He wanted to be with Barbara and his other ladies, this was where he was happy and where he knew best. It proves quite quickly that many on the spectrum do not accept change easily.

Every time he was taken to class 2 and the new teacher, he would hop it right back to where he had come from, or he would do a tour of all the classes, looking for one that was more appealing to him.

In the end, after discussion with Barbara and the head teacher it was agreed that the best place for Christopher was to stay and complete a second year in class 1.

I truly believe that not only was Chris happy but so were the teachers. So it was, Christopher did stay with Barbara, as I have already said, right up to the day she did eventually retire.

Did this make things harder for Christopher? Perhaps, but at least he had completed another useful year with a person that truly understood his needs.

Of course, with Barbara having left the school there was no option but for our son to move into class 2. Somewhere he did not want to be and with someone he had to learn to trust all over again. This was new to us as parents as well. We knew exactly how Barbara and her team worked, the support she expected from Tina and me. How would we cope with the changes? It didn't take too long to find out.

I don't know about you; it does not take me long to work someone out. Right from the start, this new teacher always had to be right. Our opinion never seemed to count. She would do things her way and any ideas, advice or help that we, as parents offered, seemed not to matter or be of any importance.

From past experience, as parents, we knew the teacher could and indeed was on a path where she would run into trouble, if she was not prepared to listen to those that knew the kids in her class better than she did herself.

There were 3 other boys in class 2, all a bit bigger than Christopher but that did not seem to bother our son. One of the habits he had started doing in class 1 was to place people, including the teachers, where he wanted them to be. He would hold them and escort each of them to the said spot. I don't for one minute think the class 2 teacher liked this and she would do all she could to prevent it happening. GOOD LUCK MISS.

The class was in fact 2 classes or one large class with a wall through the middle. I suppose at this point I should mention the new teacher's name. However, such was her impression on me and her importance to our son I cannot remember. I do remember she had a couple of support workers but generally order within the class was poor.

Unlike Class 1, that was bright and full of pictures on the walls, class 2 could be described as nothing more than an empty, drab, room that would at some point drive the best of us crazy. In the second section of the class, where the other boys seemed to spend most of their time, I think to keep them away from Chris perhaps, who had his mind made up he was to be the boss, there were a couple of small tables and chairs.

In the first section of the class, there was nothing! Nothing! Absolutely Nothing. The first time we saw this horrible looking place we were reminded of a dungeon. Who would want to stay in here?

This probably explained one of the reasons Christopher absconded at every opportunity, running into the playground and visiting other classes along the route. One class in particular that he loved to visit was decorated so brightly, just so encouraging and to top it all, one of the Barbara's that had been with him in class one was now stationed in this particular class.

So, left in class 2, what was there to keep Christopher amused, what was there he could learn. After all, he could not write anything properly, he had no desk or table to write on or a chair to sit on.

We couldn't let this go, we had to find out why the classroom was so sparse. The teacher's answer didn't surprise us, after all he had little else left to do. She told us the tables and chairs had been removed because our son had been throwing them everywhere. Was there no one in that school, a caretaker maybe, that had the ingenuity to get a few brackets, a handful of screws and make some fixings to the floor. No, instead our son was expected to sit on the floor, whilst drawing and writing.

Christopher, never to be beaten, had to have something to do with himself. He had discovered that there were live wires around the classroom walls, most of which were within his reach. Guess? Well, you don't really need to, to know what our son did next. He tore down the wires, some of which were only fixed by use of a staple gun on the hardboard walls and left them scattered around the floor. Everyone, the teacher, her helpers and the school management can think themselves lucky that there was nothing serious that happened that day. When you stop and think back, what could have been.

Let's stop a moment and consider why Christopher did this and many other behaviours that there seemed to be little or no reason. It is when you think about it, quite obvious. A behaviour is a form of communication. Quite often for someone like our son to say, no, or I don't like that. That is the time for a parent or a carer to stop and think carefully. If the child does not want something, think about why not. Think about what that child or even an adult with communication difficulties is trying to tell you. Sometimes we are all guilty of not thinking about what has just been shared with us. Why did he break that cup, why did she pour her drink all over the floor. I'll give you a really good example. Something Chris did as a very young child and before he was able to talk. He went to the fridge, took out a full bottle of milk and smashed it on the floor. He could not ask but what he actually wanted was a drink. There, a great example of how a behaviour was used as a communication tool. If you have a child that cannot express themselves, please do think about what they are trying to tell you.

Remember, the school year always starts in September, and it is not that long until October and November are upon us, often with the start of our first frosts or freezing weather. I remember one day in particular. Tina and I had to attend a regular meeting at the school with one of the therapists. We signed in and were invited to have a cup of coffee and a biscuit or two whilst we waited.

Who on earth was that shouting and screaming from outside? Why, it could be none other than our very own son. What was he doing outside when it was so cold. To get to the school and although we drove there in our car we were wrapped in warm coats, scarves and gloves, boy, it was a cold morning.

Now upon hearing what we knew was our son, we felt obliged to investigate. Shock, Horror, we could not believe our eyes. There was Christopher without a stitch of clothing on, sat in what was a puddle of water, now frozen solid, with not a soul in sight around him.

Now, of course we made a fuss, as much as was needed to rescue our son from something that could have proved so dangerous. I must say that once the head teacher was aware he ensured Christopher was wrapped up warm and ordered staff to keep a really good eye on him. Knowing that guy as I did, I bet he let rip at those teachers once we were out of earshot and quite rightly so.

Still to this very day we do not know why our son was left on his own in such a dangerous situation. Where was his teacher, where were the other support workers. Why didn't the teacher have the decency to apologise. An absolutely disgusting situation where we were left wondering if any one cared.

Something else came to mind that day and it was proper scary. What might have happened if we had not had a meeting at the school and if we had not recognised our son's shouting? How long would Chris have been left out in that playground, getting colder and colder by the minute? Perhaps another question as well comes to mind. If we had not been at the school what were the chances of the teacher being honest and us finding out exactly what had happened.

Whilst we are having a good old moan, lets tell you about something else that happened whilst Chris was in class 2. It was on a Monday morning; I remember it well. I had just dropped Chris off at the school, when I received a call from the Lodge, remember, where Chris slept every weekday until he came back home on a Friday. They were requesting some more medication and asked if I would drop it off at the Lodge. No problem, I said I would be over there soon. When I arrived at the Lodge and knocked the door I was in for a shock. As the door opened, I heard a very familiar voice and then I saw the face of my son. When I asked what he was doing there a guy told me they needed some space at school to assess two boys that were looking to join the school.

I later found out that was BUNKHAM. The truth was that as soon as I dropped Christopher at school every Monday, he was immediately taken to the Lodge and supposedly being taught there. All of this without any discussion with us and if it had not been for a request for more medication we would never have known. Why was this, could the teacher in class 2 not cope with our son and if so, why not talk to us about it.

It does make one wonder what else goes on in schools and similar establishments behind parents' backs. How do they get away with it?

Maybe, we had uncovered a very good reason why Christopher did not want to get dressed into his school uniform on Monday mornings. He just did not like going to that school anymore. What may have happened at the Lodge when he had been taken back there instead of attending the school proper? It was a real problem and to get our son to school we basically had to lie to him. Tell him we were going to the shop to buy some sweeties, then head off, via a different route to the school. That worked alright some weeks whilst others he needed a bit more convincing, maybe another little white lie. Some Mondays we would get him dressed, all ready for the off and he would decide to take off his uniform and put it all back in the drawer. You see, another behaviour, another message, further communication. Then we had to implement another plan. We went through so many but usually were lucky enough to come up with something that worked.

Pacing, just walking round and round the school playground, when he was there, or pacing around at the Lodge, that was a favourite pastime of Christopher's. He never actually seemed to care if someone was in his way, it was their place to move. Chris must have walked miles every day, no exaggeration, miles banging his feet down hard with every step. That helped with his vestibular problem, working his muscles as much as he could. Lifting heavy things would also help so Chris was often used when there was shopping to carry in or anything similar.

During the time at this school Chris had another major health problem in that his teeth were too closely packed. An absolutely lovely consultant dentist, Mrs R, her name, saw Christopher and agreed she would do the surgery herself. She was so tiny but also so special and caring. Within a few weeks Christopher was admitted, and Mrs R removed 9 of our son's baby teeth, solving a problem that could have developed into something far more complicated. Those 9 teeth are still around here somewhere, don't asked me why? Perhaps to remind us how brave our little chap was. It leaves me wondering, perhaps you as well. Why were dentists not that lovely when we were kids?

Once Christopher had developed his writing skills and remember, still at a tender age, he did not know you were supposed to choose one hand or the other to write with, he showed a very special skill where he could write with either. He would spend hours, writing great big, long lists, some would be names, others a mixture of words that he gradually added to his vocabulary. In truth, at that time he probably did not understand what many of those words meant, but somehow, by a means of genius, very few were spelt incorrectly. As his writing and reading developed you had to be especially careful of what you left laying around. You'll find out later in this book how he learnt yet another amazing skill and how he used it to his advantage. I can tell you right now what that skill was but I'm afraid you must wait a few chapters more to find out how the skill helped him out. What was it, you ask? The ability to read upside down. Now, that's got you thinking.

It was around about this same time that Christopher first showed his love for stickers, or in his terms stickys. He would spend hours peeling off stickers from books we had bought and covering cardboard boxes with as many as it took. You know during one 6-week summer holiday we bought and he transferred 36,000 stickys to their new homes. That on average was just a mere 6,000 stickys a week, fairly close to one thousand every day. You may wonder why we encouraged that sort of activity. One important reason was that it put a damper on many other behaviours, that would most probably have resulted in many more serious problems. Just think, whilst he was dealing with the stickers, he was not throwing stones, he was not smearing or throwing faeces, he was not putting biro pens in the toaster behind our backs and so the list goes on.

Recognising behaviours right from the outset and learning how to manage them is so important. It's a fact, one that I learnt from someone with whom I now have a very good friendship, born from his professionalism as a grade 5 mental health nurse and experienced when he helped looked after Chris. Thank you, Simon. I'll tell you more about this guy later.

Something we, that's both Tina and I have learnt during our journey with autism is that you must be prepared to learn more yourself. Be prepared to ask questions from those that know more. Also be prepared to deal with problems, large and small, in a calm way and showing your child plenty of love. Many is the time that Christopher has hit his mother or me or pulled our hair, but our first port of call is to look for the antecedent. What happened in the last few minutes, the last half an hour that may have pulled the trigger for Christopher. You see, once we have found what caused the bullet to be loaded, we can prevent him pulling the trigger the next time.

Looking at problems using a calm approach is the sign of a good carer, the sign of an understanding parent. We all need to aim to be better, not to blame the child, or person if it's an adult. Search for that Why, that antecedent as I said, and you have a fair chance of dealing with a potentially volatile situation in a calm and methodical way. Even professionals, teachers, carers sometimes need to remember what to do at the right time and certainly to understand what not to do.

That is why having experienced very good teachers has meant Chris has had a wonderful positive experience whilst in their class. Now let's turn that statement on its head. What sort of time does our son or anyone else's child get to experience if the teachers and carers don't have the required knowledge, that they don't have the love for their job and the ones they are supposed to be helping? There are both types out there, it is our job to sort the Wheat from the Chaff, the good and the caring from those that don't really have any special attributes.

I sincerely believe that my last paragraph makes it more than clear the difference between Class 1 and what followed. Every disabled person, whether they be just youngsters or adult, deserve the best. If you ever have to make a choice fight for the best. Do not be put into a situation where you are forced to accept whatever may be available at the time. Please remember this if nothing else. *YOUR CHILD DESERVES MORE*, they cannot possibly get that on their own. Do not rely on people like your social worker, they are under pressure to deliver, not to deliver the best. As a parent you need to take up the gauntlet and fight!

CHAPTER 3

Shame The Devil

Tell the truth and shame the Devil. A very old saying and I have no idea where it came from. I do know that my dear old mum and dad both used to drum it into me right from an early age that it was always very important to tell the truth. Perhaps because of the love my parents had for me and their determination to make sure I turned out right I learnt at a very early age not to trifle with the truth. Whenever I did the consequences were serious enough for me not to make the same mistake too often.

Now, this chapter, when you have read it right through, might put doubts in your mind whether my parents' advice was actually the best. This part of my story is going to be so hard to share as there came a time in my life where I chose to do exactly as my parents had advised and that caused Tina and I to finish up in deep murky water.

I shall never forget this period of my life, our marriage, when trust and togetherness became more important than ever before. Trust and true love in any marriage is paramount but in a marriage that has an autistic child in the mix it can become even harder. It is such a shame that sometimes for an unknown reason a marriage is doomed by the stress that autism can and will bring in almost every partnership.

It is whether, like Tina and I, you have that something special, the trust and the will to pull through no matter what the problem. In short, to put your child first, to realise that together you have more to offer and as a result more love to share between yourselves and your child.

It's all to do with a computer and a massive monitor that was connected to it that sat on a desk in the lounge. You already know, from the first two chapters that Christopher could be very destructive and indeed very quick to act once he had made his mind up. Perhaps a one-word description of our sweet little lad would be an opportunist.

I was just returning from the kitchen into the lounge when I noticed our little fella standing on the desk in the lounge already with foot raised ready to donkey kick the monitor, which incidentally had a glass front. Straight away I realised what the outcome could be if indeed he landed his bare foot in the right place and smashed the glass. The result may have meant that Chris would possibly cut himself badly, I could not allow this to happen.

It did not even once occur to me that it may also disable the monitor which of course would also put the computer out of action. It was my immediate task to get Christopher down off the desk and to prevent something that could potentially have a very serious consequence.

It was no good asking Chris to get down, that would probably only be like giving the nod to light the blue touch paper on a firework. I went straight to the problem, as such, intending to lift my son off of the desk but it was not that easy. As I put my arms around Christopher's waist he leaned over and bit me and believe me he could really bite hard. What would anyone's reaction be? Well for me it was a loss of balance and I fell backwards dropping Chris, who landed on a nearby chair, and I landed up on my son, both of us prostate on the floor. My immediate reaction was to check that Christopher was not injured and upon first sight he looked fine and had already made his way off the floor. By the time the accident happened Tina was in the lounge and had seen exactly what had happened. Like me, her concern was for Christopher, and she agreed that he did not look to have any serious injuries and was by now looking for what else he could do with his time. The main casualty appeared to be the chair. The monitor survived the ordeal, but it could not stay, we had to find an alternative.

However, by the next morning, a massive bruise had come out on Christopher's shoulder, so we had a decision to make. Do we tell the truth, shame the devil and hope that staff at the school would understand how this quite innocent accident had happened. The other choice and one that many would have plumped for would have been to keep Christopher home, make up some excuse that he was unwell and only send him back to school once the bruising had disappeared.

Guess what, we chose to call the school, even put what had happened in writing, remembering my parents' advice from all those years ago and thought that our explanation would be accepted. No such luck, you see there are too many glory hunters in this world. People that see an opportunity to score some points over you. As it stood, things between the school and us had become somewhat fractious of late, perhaps because we objected to our son being allowed to strip off in the playground on a frosty morning, maybe because of our complaints made because we found out they were secretly keeping our son away from the school and at the Lodge from the moment we delivered him on a Monday morning. It could have been any one of many reasons.

Whatever the reason, the school chose to report the matter to social services and to initiate a police investigation. One thing the school and the police didn't bank on was our other son Charlie. Remember that saying, "Out of the mouths of babes" and "children don't know how to lie". It was suggested the police speak with Charlie and that a new social worker, purely intent on growing her own reputation, might like to do the same. It was not going to go away in a hurry, but we were so proud of Christopher's brother Charlie. No messing, he told everyone that wanted to know exactly what had happened, the truth and nothing but the truth. We did later realise that as a matter of safeguarding the school had a legal obligation to report the matter. However, it was the way the whole thing was dealt with. The way everyone turned against us, not one person showing any concern about us or happening to ask how we were.

Nothing was ever proven against us, not that I or Tina would ever harm either of our boys. Neither was there any apology for what we were put through. I could, without any doubt add another five or six hundred words on this subject but believe maybe the best way forward is to put much of the problem down to other people's ignorance or perhaps lack of understanding. Most people at the school had decided not to talk to either of us, perhaps using this accident as an excuse to indemnify themselves but there was only one thing we could do after looking at the whole situation. Yes, the school had started off well, Barbara, the first teacher was a true angel towards us and Christopher. However, once things changed in class 2 and we made our opinions known, that we were not prepared for our son to have second best, everyone went on the defensive and a simple accident at home was their weapon, the excuse they needed, that they thought would be beneficial to the school and bring about our downfall.

Downfall indeed! We have had so many ups and downs in our lives since autism knocked on the door that we will never allow anything to bring about a downfall. Whenever we are threatened with a negative, we brainstorm. Both Tina and I writing down what we believe to be the answers to that particular problem. Then we think of the practicalities and work out whether we have found the right answer. If not its back to the brain storming, again the practicalities and we keep this going until we find the right answer, one that will improve things for Christopher. There is nothing else one can do if you truly care and love your autistic child, the person that is dependent up on your decisions. A

21

word of advice, always take your time making those decisions, rush nothing and ensure that your decision is good enough to last well into the future or until the decision you made is no longer practicable or serves a useful purpose.

There was only one thing we could do. Look for another school, as Chris would have said, Class 2 is Finished". There was of course a period where Chris would have to remain at that school whilst we hunted for a replacement. Our thoughts were, well it's not the first time, we have already been through this before, so we can do it again. One of the most important things we had to take on board was to make sure that wherever we chose next for Christopher, it had to be right. Don't rush any decisions, make sure social services are on board and that funding is available.

Whilst we were looking, and Chris remained at his current school it was difficult, to say the least. We found ourselves checking everything, making sure that our son was not short-changed in any manner. You could feel staff watching what you were doing, trying to listen in to your conversations. We actually avoided the school as much as possible and visited the Lodge to spend time with Christopher. Some of the staff at the Lodge were willing to chat but still there was an air of mistrust, an atmosphere between us and them.

What we hoped for was to find a new school, with boarding, in time for when the new school year started in September. It would be a push but always a possibility where we were concerned. Nothing to us was impossible, it was a case of where and when that mattered and most importantly that the "where" was 100% correct.

The end of summer term was fast approaching, which meant the annual sports day was again imminent. It would have been so easy to have stayed away on that day, but we realised this day was for our son, indeed for all of the children at the school. It was of course Christopher's last day at that school, a school like his first, that had started out so well, only to be turned upside down by one simple and yet such an important factor that seemed to happen whenever you definitely did not need it. CHANGE.

Change in staff, that was the thing that did more damage than anything else, but it is something that is inevitable, a part of the massive circle of life. As people grow to retirement, we have no right to deny them that privilege. However, I do feel strongly that some changes are made for the wrong reasons. Some people are so set in their ways, the I'll do it my way type that they won't even consider talking to parents, learning how the child ticks, what they enjoy, what they don't enjoy.

When it comes to an autistic child, there are few that know better than the parents. Just think about Tina and me. Christopher was diagnosed just shy of his third birthday, he's now twenty-four, so we have had just about twenty years of practical experience, knowing all about our son's likes and dislikes. Knowing what will cause a sudden onset of a behaviour, recognising an antecedent that could be a positive clue that something nasty or dangerous is about to happen.

So, how have we gained this knowledge, we are not particularly intelligent but have put ourselves out to find more information that will help us, with whatever autism and its traits had to throw at us. In my first book you will have read how autism specific learning started for us when Chris was very young. From the day we received his diagnosis we were searching online for anything that may help us. Then, as I wrote in Tell It As It Is, we were lucky enough to get our son on a special course called Scamp. It was an ABA course, applied behavioural analysis that meant Christopher had to attend the course for three hours every morning, three hours every afternoon, including Saturdays and three hours for good measure on a Sunday morning.

Our personal knowledge and training have increased throughout the years by literally taking on so many problems or behaviours and working out how best to deal with them. Or another source of learning has come from some of Christopher's better carers that we have met along the way. You learn from the good so you can impart that knowledge on those that don't quite have it.

One shouldn't really go naming people but when some are so exceptional, I just feel they deserve some credit. I have already mentioned in a previous chapter a guy named Simon, a grade 5 mental health nurse, that looked after Chris when he was somewhere around 15 years of age, strong by then and potentially a real handful. However, Simon never had to use any physical intervention. Even the worst behaviours were dealt with by gentle talk and gentle persuasion using very light strokes of the hand down the side of Chrissy's face. Recognising an antecedent, that was one of Simon's great assets. Knowing when to intervene, knowing sometimes when to stay quiet, to say absolutely nothing.

Then, to a little lady, named Nelli. She, too, a grade 5 mental health nurse, from the same factory as Simon. She has some very special techniques that she uses with Christopher and he, I am sure recognises her special care and appreciates everything she does. There is so much respect between Chris and Nelli and we have our own very special admiration for both Nelli and Simon and thank them for what they have done for our son and perhaps even more important and helpful, what they have taught us.

If ever you need specialist help, if any carers you are using to look after a loved one are not cutting it for you then look towards the company that trained this very special lady and young man, Thornbury Nurses. We have had the pleasure to meet so many brilliant carers over the years but unfortunately it would be impossible to name them all individually.

We want you all to know how much we appreciated the love and care that you showed to our son, how so many of you were instrumental in modelling his life, his journey through what has proved to be somewhat of a tangled web at times but one that will eventually see Christopher end up comfortable in his own surroundings.

As I said before, I try to be honest with everyone and about everything. It would therefore be wrong to leave you with the impression that every one of our son's carers were top of the ladder material. Unfortunately, there were those that were not up to the standard one would like and because of this did Christopher more harm than good. Lots of these, let say deficiencies, were delivered by agencies and had not had sufficient training and it showed in the way they cared for our son and tried to handle situations that were clearly beyond their station.

My advice to you, is always make sure what standard carers are trained to, try to ensure that any home you might choose for a loved one is not too dependent on agency staff. If staff are charged with caring for your son, daughter or maybe just a friend, don't be frightened to say something to the management if you are not happy. To do nothing, to say nothing, is letting your relative or friend down when they depend on receiving good care. Remember if you are that person's voice, do not be afraid to say something. It is not a popularity contest.

We often look towards all of these great people, the brilliant carers that Chris has been blessed with, as an extension to our family, very special people indeed, God bless you all.

I have digressed a little, sorry, it's something I am not adverse from doing. As parents and to get Chris on the Scamp course we had agree to go to the University ourselves and learn how to become two of his mentors. There were several in fact, mostly ladies that completed the team and we would take it in turn to teach, maybe train is a better word, our son. If you're not quite sure what ABA actually entails, then it's well worth looking it up but in short, it's a little bit like dog training. "Pick up that ball Rover, I'll give you a treat". Get the idea? Mind, there were days, when Chris had had enough. He'd just lay down his head on the desk and go fast asleep.

Then it was Bye, Bye mentors, see you tomorrow.

Maybe, you now understand what I am getting at. If teachers, such as the one in class 2 had just spent a little bit of their time talking with parents, the people that know the individual best, perhaps one could say they have almost professional information or opinion on their child, that teacher's job would have been made so much easier and probably would have demonstrated far better results and rewards for the individual, in this case our son.

In conclusion, I also want to say that I believe those that are supposed to work with us as parents and our children, those that have relatively well paid jobs and the title of Social Worker or similar need to set aside their ambitions of being socially above those they are paid to look after and treat them and their parents with the respect they deserve and to ensure that they make lives better. They should not need to engage in unnecessary egotistic battles just for self-gratification.

Charles Parker

CHAPTER 4

Christopher's Weekend Rituals

By the time Christopher was approaching ten years old we had found ourselves a lovely little bungalow to live in, somewhat closer to the school we were still in for now. Little did we know that in less than a year we would be hunting for another school, that could turn out to be miles away.

Just now though, I want to share what really were our son's ritualistic weekends, some of the time absolutely wonderful fun, other parts of the time he spent at home with us, could be pretty difficult.

Let's take it right from the time we picked Chris up from school on a Friday afternoon. It didn't matter too much which school he was at, as you'll gather there's been a few, Christopher's timetable was embedded well in his memory and he wasn't going to change very much for anyone.

Most Fridays, especially if Chris was at a new school both Tina and I would go to collect him and bring him home. Perhaps you can imagine, how the reception upon our arrival changed at each school, or indeed each year at any particular school as staff changed.

Just a thought that comes to mind, thinking about how many schools Chris attended during his years in education and the years beyond in the residential home and the problems he had experienced with staff. Does it perhaps prove that there is a real shortage of good, properly trained teachers and in particular carers that truly understand autism.

The first year at the specialist school, as I have already told you was fantastic and we were mostly met by Barbara on a Friday afternoon, looking very jubilant and ready to tell us about anything Chris had done during the week that she was proud of and just could not wait to tell us about.

Chris on the other hand, had one thing on his mind, dinner. It rarely ever changed, and he would start lamenting, Fish and Chips, Fish and Chips all the way to the car and again on the journey home. When you consider, that when he first went to his second school his diet was nothing more than dried cereal and chicken nuggets, he had with Barbara's help come a long way. It was also helped by our persistence and encouragement. Fish and chips weren't accepted overnight, it took time and patience. Starting with his chicken nuggets, it had to be five and they were not allowed to be touching, if they were it was a no go. Gradually, from the chicken nuggets we found other breaded foods that looked similar and that in the end Chris would accept.

Another thing that helped the transition was that Tina, little Charlie and I had fish and chips, cooked fresh in the oven, every Friday evening and as Christopher's appetite grew he needed a larger dinner. He would look across at our plates and very often point, usually at mine and say "Christophers". What a breakthrough, no problem at all. I have to confess it was a little annoying when he demanded my dinner, only to decide after pulling it apart he had eaten enough. I still remember to this day, that Chris could not immediately get his tongue around the word finished. His early version of that word was mimmished, just as his early version of Mummy was Mermaid. That really did not matter, what had been achieved was amazing, to start eating a greater variety of food was nothing short of a miracle as far as we were concerned.

Once the main course was over, the demand for his favourite and only pudding at the time was made ready, Jelly, Jelly, Jelly. In fact, a fresh jelly not only had to be made ready for when Chris got home on a Friday, but another made that night for Saturday and the same for Sunday. This actually started something where we were able to have some meaningful interaction, remember those two words, they will pop up again later in the book, with Christopher. We would start by teaching him how to break the block of jelly into cubes, then get him to stand back whilst we added just enough hot water to dissolve each block then stir in cold water to help speed up the process of setting in the fridge. Gradually, this was something Christopher asked to do, and we felt it was a job well done. One word of warning, and I should have been aware, is that when Chris broke up the jelly into smaller cubes, it was one for the bowl and one for his mouth. Exactly the same as I had done when my mother first taught me. I remember my mum when she first caught me. Why you little b….. , I'll have, your guts for garters thinking that would stop my habit. No chance.

So, we had eaten dinner, what came next? We always tried to get Chris to play outside if the weather was right, maybe help us feed the rabbits, although sometimes he was a little bit weary of getting too close. Very often though

Christopher, working off the printed copy he carried in his head, knew the next thing was bath and if that's what he demanded, that's what he got. Better to have a willing student, as they say. Sometimes, mind, Chris would be in the bath no longer than a few minutes. Guess what he would say? Bath is mimmished and he was out in a flash.

Sometimes, one could dry him off get his PJ's on and in seconds he would be saying, "What have you done"? Most times that meant he had exercised his bowels once again and it was back to the bathroom. It was, sometimes like a behaviour where he was in charge and he could call the shots, excuse the pun.

Christopher loved to watch the Telly Tubbies and because the only telly in a bedroom was in our room and we wanted to encourage him to wind down, he would sit on our bed, laughing and enjoying every minute of the show. Next was the nighttime story and generally by the time that had finished and Chris had watched every word of the credits, I do mean every word, he was close to dropping off to sleep. Only then could you suggest he go to his bed, tuck him in and hang around until he was fast asleep.

Now, think about this. The children's telly was usually finished by around 8pm and with Chris asleep we had to waste no time settling down ourselves. Eight o'clock, you say, going to bed? Not so difficult to understand when I tell you that Chris could be up by 3am demanding his breakfast. Demands came fast in the morning, breakfast, Christopher gets dressed, Christopher daddy's car. Yep, very often we would be out in the car, driving to a favourite spot by 3.30am, certainly not very often later than 4am. One also had to remember to give Chris his medication and persuading him to take that could be a nightmare in itself. Without his prescribed medication the day could potentially be very difficult indeed.

So, with Meds done, it was to the car for somewhere around seven or eight hours, stopping now and then for a toilet break, to get an ice cream and of course to top up the fuel. We went through plenty of that. Somewhere between 11 and 11.30am Chris would start going on about his lunch, always the same and always collected from the same Chippy. "Batty Sausage and Chips Daddy". They were actually so good at that Chip Shop. It just took a phone call when I was five minutes away, they would dish up the food and double wrap it ready for the journey back home. You may think that the same lunch every Saturday might become boring, perhaps you may think it unhealthy, but you try changing it. Chris would have none of it, it was his lunch, his choice and he had no intention of trying anything else.

If you had been in our house when we arrived home, you would have immediately got the impression that our son had not eaten for up to a week. His mum would plate up his Batty Sausage and Chips, that's what he called it and no matter how hard you tried to encourage Chris to slow down on the eating you were wasting your time. It seemed to be gone in seconds and if on the odd occasion I ordered something for Tina, me or little Charlie, Chris would be pointing and saying Christophers. Best was he usually won, at least one of us three gave in, perhaps if only for a bit of peace and quiet.

Now, on a Saturday afternoon, if we were lucky, we were provided with two carers. I say lucky because quite often only one would turn up, meaning that I had to make up the numbers and go along with the person that had made it.

The downside to this was that Tina and I often used those couple of hours to either do the weekly shop or take little Charlie out for a ride or a wonder along the local beach. Not much we could do to change things, we had to accept that what would be would be. It would have helped so much if the people that were meant to turn up did just that. We heard so many feeble excuses, many of which were untrue. We got used to expecting no shows especially on days when the sun was hot and the beach was probably calling.

Sometimes out of necessity we had to deliver a few orders to our customers. Yes, on top of looking after two boys that both needed very special attention, we had our own business. Tina had started it after having the boys and she was no longer able to continue her job in the insurance industry. Many of you will have heard of Kleeneze, a catalogue distribution company based on the Network Marketing system. At that time, it had been running for some 95 years.

Tina had done her investigations and found that this was something she could do, in and around our local area, taking the boys with her in a double buggy to start off with and the catalogues either on the handle of the buggy, in the basket underneath or on her shoulder. An hour or two putting the catalogues out and returning in two days to collect what was anticipated and very often was a bumper number of orders.

Tina loved it, fresh air and she was bringing in the extra pennies, whilst I was maintaining my driving school. That unfortunately came to halt in 2004, when Chris at 6 years old was getting too much for one person to handle at home. It was fine when he was at school but so much of the driving schoolwork was in the evenings and I found that I had to let people down and that was just not fair on them.

The decision was made for me to wind down the driving school and work alongside Tina with her business, me being the apprentice of course. I have to say, it worked well because whilst both boys were at school we could place far more catalogues out, hence getting far more orders in and as a result making more money. It was hard graft, lots of leg work but we enjoyed the break that it gave us both. It was an opportunity to make so many new friends, many of them elderly and glad to see us. Not only did they order products from the catalogues but often would ask us if we could pick up a few things from the shop if they could not get out themselves. We even went as far as dropping some of them at their doctor's surgery or clinic and assuring them that we would be back to ferry them home. It was so lovely, many of the customers got to know the boys and would often spoil them, perhaps showing their gratitude for our favours.

We had a number of years with Kleeneze and at the time were really making it pay. That is until they were taken over by an American, who appeared to think only of himself, and it was rumoured he had worked out how he could subsidise his own company in the U.S. using funds from our famous catalogue company. Ninety-Five years down the drain and us and thousands more left broken, no business, no income. We had to think again. It was not such a bad thing in one way, because having had a knee replacement and discovering the pain was worse after the operation than it was before meant that poor Tina had to do most of the walking, with me as her chauffeur.

Now, where was I before I told you how we made our living. Taking Christopher out on a Saturday afternoon. So, either the carers would take our son out or we would have to. He would never accept not having some sort of afternoon drive, mainly I think, because he knew he would be getting an ice-cream or ice lolly at some point. It was almost like he had a built-in clock because anywhere between 4.30 and 5pm he would start reminding the carers or us that it would soon be dinner time. The awkward part was if the carers had let us down and Tina had come out in the car with me. That meant that she could not be at home preparing and cooking the next meal. On these occasions we had to get a bit crafty. I'd drive somewhere near home but not right outside, stop and Tina would make some excuse to get out then walk the short distance home to prepare the dinner. I would drive off without explanation and use up whatever time it took my wife to get dinner on the table. That's what was expected. As soon as Christopher walked through the door dinner had to be ready.

You may be wandering what happened to our other son, Charlie, if Tina had come out with me in the car. The short answer is that my wife could only come out with Chris and me if Charlie had a carer arranged for that same day. If not, Tina would stay at home with Charlie and spend some valuable time with him. Now you're probably thinking why would Charlie need a carer? He had his own problems, anxiety and was often traumatised by his younger brother. This was recognised and a local charity group called Smile provided some help whenever possible.

Maybe a trip to the cinema, an outing to the swimming baths, indeed anything that Charlie wanted to do that would give him a break. You can no doubt see by now that autism does not just affect the one inflicted with this horrible problem, the whole family is dragged in. Charlie was lucky in that he almost always had the same carer to accompany him and therefore a trusting relationship was built up. Charlie was really no bother and was always able to hold conversations well in excess of his years, particularly if the chat was about animals or anything really to do with nature.

As Charlie grew up a little, he was eligible to attend a group called Young Carers and this again gave him relief from his brother. Charlie built up a rapport with one particular lady who had connections with a local zoo. She made Charlie's day when on one occasion she turned up with an Ostrich egg. He loved it and it still sits pride of place in the lounge. Charlie, by his own admittance, agrees he is a bit clumsy at times and did not want the egg kept in his room in case he should knock it over and have nothing left but lots of broken shell.

So, Chris has arrived home for dinner and that over it was a case of repeating everything that was part of the night before. Bath, Telly, sleep.

Something that was a real problem was the jealousy Christopher had for his brother. He did not accept Charlie around him too much meaning that Charlie was gradually forced to spend more and more time in his own room. It also meant that we had to protect Charlie from unprovoked attacks if Christopher invaded. How we prevented this happening was by screwing a piece of inch think plywood, that was as wide as the door opening and about three feet six inches high and that generally protected Charlie. So sad to think that Christopher, driven by his autism, by unexplained behaviours and jealousy saw fit to make everything as uncomfortable as he could for a brother he so obviously still loved.

So, Saturday evening, came and went without too much of a problem and left just Sunday to go to complete the weekend.

Nothing changed too much on a Sunday, Chris was still up early, ready to go for a drive by around 4am. One thing that changed was there was no Batty Sausage and chips. Tina and I are old fashioned traditionists and it was always roast dinner on a Sunday and if Chris was home that was always roast chicken, he would not try any other meat. In fact, I forgot to tell you sooner, the first thing Christopher did on arrival home on every Friday was to go to the fridge and check that mummy had bought a chicken.

Once out in the car on a Sunday morning and the time got to around 11.30am, there would be no lament about Batty Sausages, it was very clearly Roast Chicken, over and over until we arrived back home, having had the tip off from Tina that the dinner was ready and on the table. It was never gravy for Chris, he would decorate his plate with ketchup no matter what he was given.

Mealtimes were always a time when we all felt on edge. At any time Chris could be up from the table, maybe throw his plate on the floor or even attack his mum or his brother, generally by pulling their hair. I can only remember Chris pulling my hair on one occasion. However, he proved how observant he was, when I had my knee replacement operation. That was the very knee he chose to kick when he became upset one day.

He was built as strong as an oxen and before we had the seven-seater, where he would always be sat at the back and we therefore were out of range, it often brought trouble. In the car I used for driving tuition Chris was sat in the back seat directly behind the front seat passenger or in the middle seat. On many occasions he would decide to lean forward and pull his mother's hair, sometimes he would kick out at me whilst I was driving, succeeding once in breaking my shoulder, resulting in surgery. He knew exactly where to exert any attack and never once chose the wrong shoulder. We had bought a Houdini Harness, no one was ever known to get out of this; except Christopher. Oh boy! We had some fun over the years, if you can call it that but he is still your son, someone you will always love. How can you not forgive him when the first thing he says after an attack is Sorry Mummy or Sorry Daddy?

I suppose one of the worst attacks was not long after we had been forced to move from the bungalow to a three-bed house. Not our fault, the landlord and his wife had fallen out and they were selling up. There's probably more to come about life at the bungalow but I must tell you about this incident.

Christopher saw an opportunity to grab his mother's hair whilst they were both at the top of the stairs, dragged her by the hair all the way to the bottom, bumpety bump, banging Tina's back on every step. She was in agony and shortly afterwards had really bad sciatica and has never really been clear of it since. Does she still love Chris? Of course, she does, that's her baby so to speak and she knows that was the autism talking or acting not her youngest son.

It was not long after this that Tina was officially diagnosed with Fibromyalgia, a debilitating problem that haunts her to this day.

So, having digressed goodness knows how many times, we find that Monday morning has come around again and its back to school, that is if we can convince Chris to get his uniform on, keep it on and sit nicely in the car whilst we drive him back to school.   Whether we need any tricks, little white lies, that's all a waiting game, you can never guess what might happen and it's been much the same whichever school Chris has been attending over the years.

As parents, you just do what you have to. It is never for a quiet life, always for the betterment of your child.

CHAPTER 5

Holiday Rumpus and Nightmares

Now, if you think having Christopher home for a weekend was difficult or even fun very often, try to imagine what it was like having him home for six weeks.

During Chrissy's school time, some fourteen years, many of the school summer holidays were spent at home, save those when he was fifty-two-week residential care, coming home when we chose, or he asked.

Now doing some simple maths that equates roughly to ten summers that he spent at home. That's sixty weeks or four hundred and twenty days that we would have to entertain Chris, keep him safe and be responsible for him. Just think, how difficult it is when you have a "normal" child home for a few days, listening to "Mum I'm bored, Mum can I do this, can I do that".

An autistic child, even if he or she can talk a little cannot ask the regular questions and very often have to resort to behaviours, remember I said earlier, behaviours become a voice, to letting you know what your child wants, whether it be a drink, a snack, the trampoline, watch television, the list is endless and you as a parent can be drawn into a guessing game.

That is where communication, proper communication is vital: please do like we did and find out what your child might best respond to by engaging with their Speech and Language co-ordinator. With Christopher he has always responded well to using PECS, that's Picture Exchange Communication System. Having a book with lots of pictures set on a Velcro back, Chris is able to choose what he wants, show us that picture and then before he has chance to get frustrated his choice is delivered. We also use a choice board these days. A board with loads of pictures, with the writing underneath so that choices can be made whenever and wherever the need.

What we also do is a Now and Next System and each are written on a blackboard by Christopher. He then knows this is what I am doing now and what I have chosen to do next. It really does work well but is very dependent on whoever is caring for Chris at the time. Sticking to the system is vital. It is all about good timing as well, it is all VITAL, a very important word for sure when it comes to PECS and the Now and Next System.

So, that's some of perhaps what you may think boring stuff out of the way. What I want to do next is give you a flavour of what happened over the summer holidays, the fun, the stress, the excitement. I cannot possibly tell you everything that happened through every holiday but I sure as heck can bring you some things that I hope you'll never forget for the right reasons.

Let's start at the bungalow, not long into the summer holiday. Down the end of the garden was the most amazing old apple tree. I would hazard a guess that it was somewhere between fifty and one hundred years old. Not long after we had moved in fell in line with the end of the fruit season that particular year and so it was a good time to prune the tree, getting rid of a whole lot of dead wood and so encouraging new growth. That time was well spent, the tree this year following my rather harsh haircut was loaded. Hardly surprising as there had been masses of bloom a few weeks earlier and with the number of bees on duty pollination was at a premium. Are we already, I said to the family, let's get these apples picked, some had to be knocked down and some were fallers. The idea was to get the whole job done in a day or so. The tree was a Bramley, ideal cooking apples and great for the freezer. First a warning and this was difficult to communicate to Christopher, if you pick fruit from the floor look out for resident bees. We tried to encourage Chris to wear gloves, but our idea was not taken well. We would just have to keep a good eye on him and the busy insects, working their way through the fruit.

One of the fun bits was knocking the fruit off the tree and onto the grass below. We had a great long stick, two pieces of wood nailed together that was just long enough to reach the top. We also found a couple of shorter sticks so that both Charlie and Chris could reach some of the fruit and have the fun of knocking them down. One small problem was convincing Chris that the sticks were only for hitting the fruit and not his brother. Fortunately, he soon got the message when Charlie retaliated and demonstrated how much it could hurt.

It was truly amazing how Chris cottoned on to the idea, even helping to hold, the longer stick and laughing as each apple fell to the floor, dodging out of the way where needed to avoid a bump on the head. As soon as he saw we were then picking the fruit up and loading it into whatever bags, boxes or bowls were available he was into that as well. It was wonderful, we were a family, working together and most importantly enjoying the time, just having fun. Of course, Christopher could not resist delivering a few of the apples to the neighbours' gardens but I just could not think of a good reason to spoil his fun and there were plenty to go around. I believe that year we harvested over eighty pounds of fruit. That fruit then had to be prepared for the freezer.

Peeling, chopping and blanching the fruit would take quite a while but with Tina and me taking it in turns to peel and chop, whilst the other looked after the boys meant we had everything done over the course of the next couple of days. The harvest complete and stored ready for the winter.

Something else Chris liked to do was hide away, somewhere quiet, somewhere that was his, so we bought him a pop-up tent, just about big enough for him to get in and he loved it. Then came the fun, when Chris insisted that daddy should also get into the tent and help him with some writing and drawing. We spent hours in his beloved red tent until one day he decided enough was enough and he busted it up. "What have you done" he said, "poor tent".

Other things that Chris did in the garden was to wind the neighbours Jack Russell dogs up. He thought it was great fun, when the dogs were laid down, nice and quiet, for him to run up and down on our side of the fence making his doggie noises. Woof, Woof, followed by endless laughing. Although the neighbour had made it clear he completely understood autism, as his wife worked with children like Chris, I am not sure he was best pleased.

Perhaps something that confirmed our suspicions was when we had bought the boys a large and very lovely bouncy trampoline. Both Chris and Charlie loved the idea of bouncing up and down but would not often spend time together on it. One of Christopher's best tricks was to give Mummy and Daddy the run around when it was time to go in doors and get ready for bed. Whilst he had a sort of bedtime or after dinner ritual the trampoline was the one thing, he was reluctant to leave. He would stand in one spot, wait for you to run around to where he was and at lightning speed he would be gone across the other side. I think he was well aware that having had a knee replacement I was not able to either run around or climb on to the trampoline to get him heading in the right direction. If his mum braved it and climbed on, he was clever enough to know that if he jumped high enough or hard enough, he could cause her to fall over. He would then keep jumping making sure that mum had no chance of regaining her footing. It was then of course a case of hanging it out and eventually catching Christopher off guard.

For a man who by his own confession told us he understood autism the neighbour showed little proof of this by two things that he did. First, he raised the garden fence on his side so that it was ten feet tall. Ten feet, and therefore cutting much of the light from our lounge. Now, I thought, shall I point out that he is in contravention of the ancient light laws of the land, stretching back hundreds of years, perhaps make an official complaint so that he had to make further adjustments, causing more expense for him or shall I use this monstrous fence to our advantage. At ten feet it meant that we could not see him and in turn he could not see us. Have you guessed? Both Tina and I simultaneously decided on the latter. We figured that whilst the fence caused us one or two problems, that it was probably doing exactly the same to him and his wife. What's that saying. "Honi soit qui mal y pense". Or in good old English, "Evil Unto Him That Evil Thinks". I often thought of that phrase when I looked at his fence or heard his voice on the other side.

As if that was not enough, that same man, the person that understood all about autism, was on the war path again. Word got back to us that he had produced a petition, gone all around the neighbourhood and asked people to sign. The petition was to get us forcefully removed from our home, to be rehoused in a more appropriate area. I have great news! No one, not one person signed that petition. I repeat, "Honi soit qui mal y pense".

Perhaps one lady that had every right to sign was a lovely person that lived right opposite our bungalow. During the summer holiday we were lucky enough to get some respite, a couple of hours on a Sunday afternoon. The carers turned up right on time. They were relatively new to Chris and we reminded them that they should link arms with Chris, one either side, to see him safely to the car. Did they listen? No! As soon as they were outside of our front door Christopher was off. Neither of the carers had any contact with our son. It was clear why Chris did what he did next. He had looked across the other side of the road where it was houses, not bungalows and he had seen a front door wide open. The carers had no chance, and as for us, all we could do was shout and hope he would listen. No hope. Christopher was in the front door, up the stairs, into the lady's master bedroom, where a brand-new bed had been delivered that very morning.

A bed, what is a bed to an autistic child, if it's not for sleeping in. Why it's an indoor trampoline and Christopher was onboard in the blink of an eye. Now, fortunately, the lady of the house was not like the lovely man that lived next door to us. She was aware our son was autistic, understood what that meant and before we had any chance to chastise the carers, she gave them the biggest telling off they had probably ever had to endure. She made it very clear, it was their fault and that if they wanted a future in the caring industry they must first learn to listen to parents, the ones that know best. Bless that lady, she was so understanding. By the way, for some reason, she never left her front door open again. Any idea why?

So far, I have covered things that happened whilst we were living at the bungalow but what you must remember is that Chris didn't really know one day from another. The only differences that stuck in his mind were whether he was at school or at home. If he was at home, it meant that he expected to follow his usual routine. That meant that he was up very early and expecting me to drive him out, not just on a Saturday and Sunday but every day. Anything else we had planned had to be fitted in around the drives out. It also meant that Chris expected the same lunch almost every day, Battie sausage and chips. Now, one thing you may not have worked out is that chip shops are no longer cheap. Around about £3.50 a day, so six days and you are looking at £21 a week and of course that is only Chris's lunch.

The holidays, as you can guess quickly became very tiring, I'm not quite sure where we found the energy from some days, but we made it.

Living at, the bungalow was great but because of the battle with the neighbour we were not entirely upset when our landlord turned up at the door one evening. We knew right away it would be something serious as we hadn't seen him since the day we moved in, just the odd phone call now and then. He was so apologetic as he broke the news. He and his wife were breaking up and the bungalow had to be sold and the profits shared. We felt sorrier for him I think, especially when he explained that his wife had been playing away. He was clearly heartbroken but relieved at how we had taken things. He told us to take our time, to find the right place and to let him know when we were moving out. He could not be any fairer to us than that.

This may shock you but within days of being told we had to move out I had potentially found a new place where we could move in. Less than a mile from the bungalow. I just happened to be driving in towards town and I spotted a board up outside a house, saying ready soon, with the name and number of an agent. Blow it, I thought, I'm going in. So, I stopped and did just that, called out to a builder and asked if I could have a look around. Having done so and being pleased with what I saw my next move was a call to the agent. He happened to be in soul control as the elderly owner lived in Sri Lanka. Without much further ado a deal was struck, deposit paid and all we had to do was wait for the work to be finished.

Once we knew a moving in date, we kept our word to the owner of the bungalow and told him when he could have the property back. He was actually quite amazing, he gave us a great covering letter, one that he advised us to keep and use at any time we needed it.

So, we got the family booked, that is son, daughter grandkids that were old enough to help and booked a van. Moving can of course be traumatic but by the time our day came round both Charlie and Chris were back at school and the day went well. After all, it was only a short drive and it took longer to load and unload the van than it did drive the distance between the two properties.

When Christopher came home on the next weekend it was chaotic. He had not had stairs at the bungalow and so had to run up and down the stairs as many times as possible just to get in the groove.

The garden was so different, one massive slope, going uphill away from the house and Chris had to explore this ready-made gym at every opportunity. One thing we had to do was have a side gate fitted to stop the young man escaping.

By the time we had moved into the house Chris was back at school and only coming home at weekends. By the time another year had passed, and another summer holiday was upon us Chris was again home for the whole six weeks. I don't really want to tell you why that came about, at least not until a bit later.

One of the big differences between the bungalow and the house and not the obvious one about an upstairs, whilst at the house, it was a little more in the form of open plan. One could walk into the kitchen from the lounge and walk out the other end of the kitchen and be back into the lounge again. Christopher loved this, it was like a mini running track, round and round he would go, never showing signs of tiring himself out.

Of course, one of the downsides of the house and an open kitchen is that Chris could go into it whenever he wanted to, often turning on the cooker, placing CDs in the toaster and pens or light bulbs if he came across something like that in the microwave. This was so dangerous, the house could so easily be set on fire and whenever you caught Chris at any of these games, as I'm sure that's what they were to him, you would be greeted with another of his wry smiles.

What could we do about this, how could we make the home safe again? I decided to seek the help of a professional who said the only answer was to have an isolator switch fitted, out of Christopher's reach and that we must try not to make it obvious. That's a joke, I thought, don't make it obvious. Chris has eyes everywhere and whilst we thought our secret switch was still that, a secret, I'm sure Chris knew what we were doing as we finished using the cooker, or any of the other electrical equipment and I am sure he had spotted us turning the main switch on. You see, being shorties, my wife and I had to use a broom handle to flick the switch. As Chris grew, what we spotted was a young man able to reach easily as high as the isolator switch and beyond. He thankfully had not quite realised, just yet anyway, how to make the switch work.

Christopher had so many more tricks up his sleeve, we would need to continue at the top of our game.

Perhaps to give you an idea of how vigilant one had to be, let me just give you a couple of his worst behaviours that without doubt Chris knew would wind us up and test our patience to the limit.

Our son found it great fun, when he felt the need to urinate and rather than use the toilet, to dash off upstairs and wee over the banister, giving you both a shock and the need for a shower if you were not alert.

Another behaviour, I am sure he knew would be difficult for us to resolve was to load his hand with faeces and toss it onto to the ceiling on the stairs. Look at your own stairs now and you will quickly see how high up that ceiling is and how difficult it was for us to reach up there and clean up the mess.

Most difficult was not to make a big thing of these behaviours and if you did you were inviting that innocent little chap to do the same over and over again.

One had to be pretty alert out in the garden as well, for Chris, not keen on touching the rabbits, would sometimes open a hutch, grab a bunny by its ears and release it onto the garden floor. If you were not there to see it happen, which fortunately most times we were as we were intent on caring properly for our boys it would be easy for the rabbit to go anywhere in the garden, or indeed next door, once it found a few small holes in the fence. The alert, always raised of course by Chris saying that familiar phrase, "What have you done"? Thank you, Chris.

So, before I started the last couple of chapters, I mentioned Christopher's last day at the school that was fairly local to us. Now, if one school ends, another has to start, but it's not that easy. The search has to go on as soon as you know it's necessary. With the demise at the so-called specialist school happening fairly quickly we did not have loads of time to search, to get the placement approved and a successful transition completed, before the next school year would start.

Let's waste no time, I'll move on to the next chapter and tell you how we got the change of school sorted.

CHAPTER 6

Holiday Inn or the Hilton

So here we are again, searching. Searching for what we hope will be the answer to our prayers, a school that can look after our son successfully and that has the room.

Then of course the big question, will the school we find be approved by the local authority. Will the funding be made available?

We knew time would tell and this time around we did not have an abundance of that. It was to be no easy task. As Chris grew older, he became more difficult and would need more specialist staff with a vast experience and knowledge of autism. This is something that was thankfully recognised by the local authority at that time but fast forward many years, when we had to find care for Chris when he started Supported Living and it was so different. You'll discover what I mean a little later in the book.

We knew that Chris would finish at the current school at the end of the summer term, a couple of months away and we also knew that would fly by. If we were to find an appropriate school, that also offered residential care we must get a shift on. Maybe we would have to look further afield, we could think of nothing in and around our home city of Southampton. If that meant moving further afield to find a placement that would benefit Christopher, it didn't really matter, we would look anywhere for the right place and if necessary up sticks and move ourselves to anywhere that would make things better for him.

What we must do this time around is to make sure we ask all the right questions, please or offend. Be polite but be thorough. The truth is that management at the schools Chris had been to so far always appeared very polite at the start. Was that perhaps because Christopher, like many of the modern-day footballers carried with him an enormous transfer fee so to speak. I'm more than sure that at least one of the schools or the care home our son has been at saw nothing more than money when they did their assessment. You'll probably work that one out for yourself, so read on.

It is indeed so appalling, that any establishment, whose sole task is to offer a safe home, an education and indeed a happy future to a venerable person is guided solely by how much profit they could make by accepting them through the doors. Generally, as each child with autism moves through the system the cost of care goes up and up. In Christopher's early school days the cost was almost like a secret, like the Local Authority were doing you a favour but you're not going to know how much it's costing.

Let's give you an idea of just how much Christopher was worth to a school. At the first specialist school they probably received something between £100,00 and £130,000, that's an educated guess. At the next school that we found and got Chris into we found out that they benefitted by around £180,000 a year, staggering is it not. That was in fact a school in Dorset, a residential school sitting fairly near to an airport, in Bournemouth and some thirty miles away from home at the time.

So let's tell you how we got on with this search, join us as we look for what is next, what we consider the best, and what we decided we thought was best for our son.

There are two ways to find decent residential schools, the first being, to ask around, perhaps use Facebook and your friends and the second is to get on to the internet and start searching.

We had tip offs about two residential schools, one in the New Forest and the other as I said in Dorset, that being the one we eventually decided upon. No others anywhere near Hampshire appeared to be available. It was now down to us to sort the wheat from the chaff, so to speak. Which of these two schools would take our eye, which had the most to offer?

Taking the lazy way out to start off with we looked at each school on the internet. Sometimes it's hard to make your mind up looking at pictures but with these two schools there was already a clear runner. We thought and knew, it was a big decision, we had to get this right. It wasn't far to drive to either, perhaps forty minutes or so and being very impetuous we were in the car and on our way as soon as we had taken our afternoon tea and biscuits.

Now, here's where I digress again. Tea and biscuits, nothing beats it in the middle of the afternoon. I clearly remember when Chris was at home one afternoon, Tina had made the tea and I was dunking. Almost immediately Chris got the message, grabbing a couple of biscuits, with a polite "Please Mummy" and finding out for the first time the enjoyment of tasting a digestive and a ginger freshly dunked in daddies' tea. That now happens every time he is around, and tea and biscuits are on the menu. One problem of course, is that Chris doesn't always have the right knack, holding the bickie in the cup too long and then it turns to crumbs at the bottom. There is nothing worse and Tina laughs every time it happens, she thinks it an appalling habit. I have overcome that by making Chris his own cuppa and he has the time of his life.

So, tea and biscuits done with, we set out in the car to the first of the schools, the one farthest away in Dorset. By the time we reached the area, it was almost rush hour and the traffic around the airport was extremely heavy. The last mile or so must have taken close on an hour, stopping and starting every few minutes. No matter, we had to see this school, would it really live up to what we had seen on the net.

Eventually, we arrived. The school was on a very busy road and there was little room to pull in anywhere safely, without blocking the main gates, that appeared to be controlled by some sort of electronic intercom system. "We can't stop here long", I remember Tina saying. I wanted to get as good a look as possible, take everything in, you know what they say about first impressions. Almost everything, the gates, the doors looked to be freshly painted, all looking very impressive.

"Hey Tina", I said with an air of excitement in my voice, "that building over there must be the swimming pool that we saw online".

It looked just amazing and although we had been parked outside for just about fifteen to twenty minutes, we were very close to being sold on the idea. Already the caution we had promised ourselves to exercise, to take our time and be very careful, had all but disappeared. At first, we were all for getting home and calling the school to arrange a viewing but realised we still had another school that we must go and take a look at.

The first couple of miles back toward the forest were as slow as the last two, about thirty minutes before. Never mind, one down one to go. After about fifty minutes we approached Lymington and then on to a tiny village called Boldre where our second viewing was waiting. Again, we had not made any arrangement to go into this school, just a quick look from outside to give us some idea.

We drove down the single-track driveway and there almost hidden away was the school. First impressions, "look at the state of that place". How could we ever think about sending our son there? The title chosen for this chapter says it all. "Holiday Inn or The Hilton? In my mind and I am sure at that time Tina was of the same impression, it had to be the Hilton for our Chris.

45

Our minds were made up, The Hilton it was! That is, if they had any places available for the next term. We made sure to make the phone calls both to the school and the local authority the very next day. Two different types of call, never any different. The first, a new school, sounding really excited, warm and welcoming, possibly already counting the pennies that our son would be worth to them. Then the second call to the Local Authority. No excitement here, that's for sure. The usual droll boring voice, "We will have to see", What's wrong with the school he is at?" Then carrying on, "We are not sure if your choice of school is appropriate and not sure if the budget will allow this to happen". "You'll have to put your request in writing".

I tell you, there were no surprises, we had heard it all before. Tell me any Local Authority that wants to part with more money? That's their number one consideration. Not, is this school going to be better for the young man? Is this school more likely to be able to handle his behaviours, by moving him from a school that clearly cannot cope, will there be any benefits? The list could go on.

Well, we were told to put the request in writing and we did, the very next day, right after calling the school, introducing ourselves and finding out that they did have room for our son. Also arranged at the same time was a visit to the school to take a look inside and out and to ask dozens of questions. Boy was the pen busy and the paper taking a hiding on the day we took our look around.

The actual visit was amazing, everyone so polite, a fish and chip lunch included and an outline of how the school worked, firmly in our mind. The visit took place as I remember in June with an aim of Christopher starting in September. Not long, especially when you take on board the speed and efficiency of the council. There would need to be many phone calls and letters written to get everything done on time. Don't worry, we had done this sort of thing before, and we were up for it again.

One thing, however, stalked my mind. Had we gone for the right school? Was the Hilton the right place? With the time we had left it was almost too late to change our mind and we still had to push this move through let alone think about another.

There were many meetings with the school, the authorities and people like the educational psychiatrist, who played a very big part in getting everything signed off. Mind the authority, made us wait to the very last moment. They didn't really care, it wasn't their child, what difference would it make to any of the powers to be. I really do believe that they think of the bank balance first before ever thinking about what the child needs, maybe how a parent needs support, you know what I mean, giving help where it is truly going to be appreciated.

On one of our visits to the school, I noticed some horses in the adjacent field and suggested to Tina that perhaps they were the ones the children got to ride. We had read it was something that was encouraged with some students, although I had my doubts about Chris, he was nervous around any animals. Time would tell of course.

The dates were set for Chris to visit the school, for him to find out if he liked it and indeed for the school staff to find out how they could cope. Trials out of the way, the big day was approaching, Chris was off to his new school. We drove in through the double gates on the Monday morning and we were greeted by a lady that was to be our son's new teacher. She really genuinely did feel lovely. It was immediately apparent that patience was something she had in abundance. Patient and yet firm, that's how I would describe her. Mind, I am not quite sure she truly knew what she had let herself in for, again time would tell.

We stayed in touch with the teacher throughout the week and anxiously waited for Friday to arrive, when we would drive down to Dorset and collect our angel. Chris was brought back to the car by the same lady that had collected him and quite surprisingly it appeared that they had already forged a pretty good relationship. Chris was so happy to see us both and could not wait to get into the car and repeatedly tell us where he wanted to go. HOME! HOME! HOME!

As Chris would have little understanding why he had to wait for his dinner, Tina had prepared everything and as soon as we arrived home she put the oven on full heat, ensuring as little time as possible was wasted between arriving home and the food being presented on the table. Wow, that was a big day, a big week, a new start for our son that we hoped would continue in a fantastic way.

One of the things we were looking forward to as a family was joining Chris in the school swimming pool and we were able to do so after a couple of weeks. It was great fun and we were assured we could use the pool on as many visits as we wanted, provided we booked in advance. What we didn't realise was that our opportunities would quickly become few and far between. It seemed that every time we wanted to use the pool with Chris, someone from an outside group had the pool booked. It soon became obvious that the school pool was being used as a fund raiser. Children at the school, including Christopher were allowed to have their time in the pool but when it came to us spending time as a family that was out of the question. Never mind, we just hoped that the rest of the time at the school for Chris would be very positive.

As the weeks in Year One went by everything seemed to be working out well. Each Friday we would be pleased to hear a positive response from the teacher. She appeared to be a bit like Barabara, remember Christopher's first teacher at his previous school. No messing, that was her policy, but she always seemed to be fair and have an expectancy of our son that was attainable. It is how people present themselves to our son that will often be the deciding factor in whether they are accepted by Chris or whether he decides he wants little to do with them.

One thing that Christopher did make decisions on was where other students in the class would sit or stand and perhaps ever more surprising where the teacher and her helpers were to fit in with our son's ideas. This was again just like he had done at his previous school.

Chris continued to make progress throughout that first year, we delivered him to the school on a Monday morning, visited him every Wednesday evening and took him for a ride to you know where, Mac Daws and then of course collected him on a Friday afternoon. He knew by the time he was safely in the car exactly what his weekend must look like, what he would eat, where he would go, no week ever very much different but that was what pleased our lad.

Time raced away, Christmas came and went and it would not be too long when we had to think about year two. What would that hold, year one at all of Christopher's schools had been completed fairly well, whilst the second year at the same schools had brought so much disappointment. We knew Chris would be in a new class and would definitely have a new teacher as the one he had for the last year was moving on, promotion at another school. Good luck to her, she deserved it, she knew her job.

We also had heard that the lady, the acting head, who had held the fort pretty well was to be upstaged by a man, who in fact was also a director and on the board of the school management. I shall however refer to him as the head teacher. Could we at long last afford to have some optimism as to the future in year two of a school that Christopher was attending. We shall see.

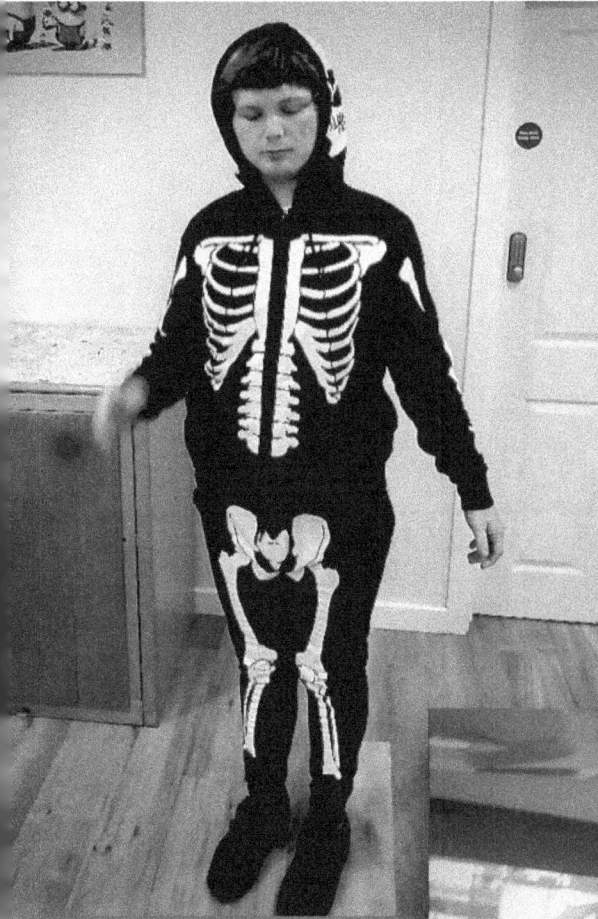

Left: *Halloween - at the residential home 2018*

Right: *In Daddy's car on route to Mac Daws*

Right*: Working on a pumpkin.*

Left*: Chris and his Dad in the New Forest - Just as the sun was rising.*

CHAPTER 7

The Second Year

Wow it has happened again!

To date, Chris had already attended two other schools and now at the third. In each of his schools, the first year was not too bad. Was it the NEW BROOM SYNDROME? Goodness knows. Staff just came across as being so lovely, so co-operative and willing to help Chris make strides forward.

By the time Christopher reached the second year in Dorset things were happening that clearly should not have done and much of the demise or lack of care was somehow being laid firmly with us as parents.

One massive change, as I mentioned in the previous chapter was in the leadership. The lady that had been Acting Head had left and had been replaced by a man, who right from the start gave the impression that what he said would go, he was always going to be right. For now, anyway, I will leave his name out and continue to refer to him as the Head Teacher, perhaps a Nasty Piece of Work, might be more appropriate.

At this school Chris started off as a weekly border and by year two was a fifty-two-week resident. There wasn't much time where he was at home and where we could have influenced his behaviour.

I make no secret that matters had certainly started to dip by the start of the second year and by the end of that year everything was in free fall, but I suppose one must always live in hope.

At the end of the summer term in the second year we were invited to a school assembly and presentation where to our surprise Christopher was given the award for the child making the most progress. So hard to believe, we could not understand quite why.

Then at the end of the presentation, with us thinking Chris would be staying there for the summer holidays we were shocked to be handed a letter, written by the head teacher telling us that Christopher had been expelled from the school. Angel one moment, devil the next. How strange, that the school had waited until it had received the funding to cover the summer holidays and with this in the bank, so to speak, they could go ahead and remove our son.

What did that mean? That Christopher's time at that school was finished, it was now time to start looking again. Taking a phrase from a very prominent actor, I said to Tina, "I don't believe it!"

Once again, we had found a school, incapable of looking after our son, teaching him in a manner that showed little if any improvement and perhaps most importantly keeping him safe. This particular time was certainly to be a part of Christopher's life that we wish had never happened, both for his benefit and ours as parents. Psychologically, our son still suffers mental recall from his time at that school. We can be out in the car with him even now and he will suddenly start talking about his time at Dorset, naming the school and lamenting how he witnessed his friends being illtreated. It is not in detail, just simple English if you like but the message is there.

I want to beg your forgiveness at this point. With that school going downhill so fast we had to find somewhere else and very fast. What I want my readers to experience is the truth about what happened to our son during his stay there however, particularly the second year. As there was an urgency about getting Christopher moved, I had, before getting the letter excluding him, felt it necessary to prepare for what would almost certainly lead to an inevitable tribunal. You see, the Local Authority had only a year or two previous agreed for our son to be moved from one bad school and now we were saying we want to do the same again and for many of the same reasons, some even worse.

I prepared the tribunal papers and now find myself wanting to bring you more or less the same information. The following is some of the evidence that my wife and I prepared, I trust it will not shock you too much. I suppose some good news is that there now would be no need for a tribunal, we haven't withdrawn our son he had been kicked out. However, I will share with you much of what went on in that second year.

As parents we were invited to behaviour meetings held at the School but became frustrated that most of the time was spent discussing or criticising the management of our son at home. It made us feel that the only time he misbehaved was at home. We decided to ask at one of the meetings if we could have copies of reported incidents at school, both in the educational setting and residential setting. It is without any doubt that we were truly amazed when we received these figures and thought I would take the liberty of sharing them with you. We have looked at each of the incidents and marked them according to their seriousness. We used Green for non-contact behaviours, shouting, swearing, smearing and stripping. Blue was used to mark any self-harming. We split what we considered to be Serious incidents into four categories and used Red and numbers one to four. Number one for general serious incidents, number two for damage to property, number three injuries to others and damage to property and finally number four represents very serious incidents including injury to members of the public, serious injuries to others within school, serious damage to property and finally and most importantly Attempts to Abscond. In number four all of the incidents recorded with the exception of two represented attempts to Abscond.

Obviously, I am unable to show my findings using colours in this book, but I mention it just in case a reader needs to conduct a similar study.

	In 2012 (240 Days)	In 2013 (147 Days)
Non-Contact Behaviours etc.:	71	26
Self-Harming/Anxiety	34	258
Serious	41	16
Damage to Property	77	42
Injury to others	161	78
Abscond attempts/Injury to Public	16	8
Injury to Public	2	
TOTALS	402	428

When we presented our findings for 2012 to the School the behaviour specialist stated that our findings were not accurate. That many of the incidents were not serious. We beg to differ. Any incident that involves a child self-harming is in itself serious and the cause of each incident should be explored. However, incidents involving damage to property or injury to another person is extremely serious and questions must be asked why the incident occurred.

The question must also be raised that as Christopher had two to one care at all times how it was possible to harm others or do so much damage to property if those carers were paying attention to our son. Evidence that in our opinion proved staff were not paying enough attention is given herewith. On studying many of the incident forms it would appear that carers were leaving our son on his own, particularly in his bedroom. We questioned why Christopher was not receiving two to one care at all times. He is unable to structure his own time and if left he will look for a negative way to gain attention. Unless asleep he should not be left at any time. At home we are with Christopher all of the time until he is asleep. We do not believe that showing him DVDs late in the evening, in his bedroom and on his own is a good idea.

We asked the school management to refer to two of the incident forms that mention Chris chose to shred up many items of clothing and bedding. If efforts to understand Christopher were worked on so many of his behaviours would have been eliminated. Lots of meetings were held at home with the clinical psychologist. These meetings proved to be successful and between us many situations were dealt with. As parents we would be the first to admit that not everything goes well but we learn by our mistakes and if we change the way behaviours are dealt with it would ensure improvements for our son. One very positive matter was resolved by the clinical psychologist. That in his professional opinion our care of Christopher at home was exemplary and at a meeting at the school he made that very clear.

Here are some questions we put to management at the school. Needless to say answers were not forthcoming.

Why did staff not distract or intervene when our son trashed the first of his bedrooms at Portfield? Put another way, why were they always Reactive rather than Proactive?

Why, when a screwdriver was left in his bedroom did neither of his carers notice it and stop him from totally wrecking his bedroom? An autistic child in the procession of a dangerous tool could have done untold damage to himself or others. It would not be beyond Christopher pushing the screwdriver into the electrical points and electrocuting himself. We had to make a fuss at two meetings to ensure remedial work was carried out. Until then the bedroom was left a disgrace and a danger to our son.

Why, when Christopher accessed the sensory room and wrecked many of its features did the carers, bearing in mind they were supposed to be with him at all times do not intervene and stop him from doing the damage. This facility since then was made unavailable for other service users, for a considerable time.

Why, when he apparently hit himself in the face, causing swelling and a very large bruise did neither of his carers intervene or distract our son? It must be noted that as parents we were not informed of this injury at the time or before our next visit. It was left to us to notice the serious injury on our next visit and ask his carer what had happened. She said "Oh haven't you been told, I'll get the paperwork.

No paperwork was available and to this day we have not received an incident form relating to this injury. However, the school maintains that Christopher did inflict the injury on himself, something to this day we question. We have tried to inflict such an injury on ourselves and found it almost impossible to produce enough power from a short distance. We produced a photograph, taken on the evening of our visit, to a senior nursing sister and she doubted whether Christopher could possibly have caused the injury to himself.

Another cover up by the school, and the injury was not reported to the Social Worker or Safeguarding. We informed the social worker after our visit. The Social Worker then took the issue up with the school and asked their nurse for an opinion. We believe due to the extent of the injury Christopher should have been seen by an external doctor with no relation to the school. Such was the seriousness of this injury; the social worker asked the school to look at their child protection procedures and we thank her for that.

- Why were there 402 incidents in 2012, 73.8% were serious and 44.5% very serious?

- Why had there been 428 incidents in 2013, 33.6% serious and 21% very serious?

- In the first six months of 2013 there were more incidents than in the whole of 2012.

- Why had there been an enormous increase in self-injurious incidents from 2012 to 2013?

- In just eighteen months (387 school days) there were 830 incidents.

Just to make it easier to envisage the amount of incident forms, think about this. We had asked the school to produce a copy of every incident form that had been written about our son. We were shocked one day when a parcel arrived. It was a box, that would normally hold five reams of paper, that's two thousand, five hundred sheets and the box I speak of was full to the brim. We were so glad we asked for them and to this day, the box complete with the forms, sits in our shed, just in case, as they say.

As parents we were very concerned that the number of incidents involving self-injurious behaviour has risen from 8.45% in 2012 to 60.28% over the first six months of 2013. We believe this may have meant that Christopher was not happy at the school. We also believe it could have been because his skin irritation had not been managed properly. If, when Christopher is at home, there is any sign of his skin becoming inflamed (He has problems with Hives and Eczema and still has lasting effects from Scarlet Fever) we immediately administer the prescribed medication. We also apply Hydrocortisone cream to the affected areas twice daily as instructed. We do not believe this happened on a regular basis. There were times when we had been visiting Christopher and observed him becoming irritated and scratching himself. We then suggested to the school that they give him his medication.

One week we received an email updating us of Christopher's behaviour in the residential setting. Over the course of the week, he had kicked several holes in the playroom walls. We would suggest that it was Christopher's way of expressing he is unhappy. We would ask also where the carers were during each incident.

When collecting Christopher from school one Friday his teacher, reported that Christopher had been difficult and had kicked two holes in the walls of the classroom. The teacher also believed that the behaviour was a roll over from residential and that he was worried that the behaviour would continue on the Monday when Christopher returned to school.

We cannot understand why Christopher was allowed to attack and often hurt staff and other service users. Why were incidents allowed to reach that point? We wonder if Christopher attacked staff because he is not happy or had one or more of the staff ill-treated him in the past. We also believe that if his skin irritation had been managed properly the number of attacks on persons would have fallen dramatically. On many of the serious incidents, some witnessed by us, Christopher was surrounded by three, four and sometimes five carers. According to the educational psychologist, the more people you put around any child the worse you will make them.

The answer must be to manage the behaviour in a positive manner from the outset and not allow it to escalate. We have witnessed occasions when Christopher has asked staff for something, and they have ignored his request.

We have spent lots of our time worrying about the safety and security of our son. In just one year there were more than twenty attempts to abscond from school by Christopher. The question that must always be asked is why? We, believing it is because he is unhappy, but also would be hard to prove. Possibly not happy with some members of staff. The number of times that Christopher has made suggestions that certain staff have hurt him, makes this idea possible and quite likely realistic.

We are of the opinion that every attempt to abscond is Christopher using the only means of communication he knows to demonstrate he is not happy. One evening we witnessed one of his attempts to abscond, caused because none of the three carers accompany him to our car had linked their arms with him. In fact, the main reception door of the school was wide open, as were the perimeter gates and Christopher ran out of the door some ten to fifteen yards in front of the carers and he made straight towards the gates.

It was only the quick thinking of his mum, Tina, having heard him coming and got out of our car in preparation, that prevented a possible nasty accident. She managed to dash across towards him, cut him off and grabbed his shirt and redirected him to our car. It was not only our son we have witnessed running away. On another of our Wednesday evening visits we had entered the main gates and, on our way, to collect our son we witnessed a boy alight from a school bus, without any carer holding him and he immediately ran off in the direction of the gates. We stopped our car as a matter of safety. The child ran across the front of our car. The whole incident caused real worry and concern to our other son Charlie who had come with us to visit his brother. The carer supposed to be with the boy had no chance of catching him and eventually called for two other helpers to assist in catching the child. If another vehicle had arrived or one wanted to leave, and the main gates had been opened that child could have bolted on to a main road. The problem with Christopher running off was caused because none of his three carers had looked thoroughly at and worked in accordance with his risk assessment. Instead of being Pro-Active they were Re-active. This would seem to be the problem every time. At home we plan for his weekends and try to envisage what might go wrong and have an answer to that problem ready to put into place.

Again, I ask, why were there twenty-four attempts by Christopher to abscond from that School in 387 days. This included some attempts from public areas whilst out with staff. That averaged out at one attempt every sixteen days.

Chris had broken out of Parley One, where he slept, on many occasions, run to the trampoline area, stripped off, messed himself, smeared over the trampoline and then run towards the main gate that was open at the time.

To this day I still wonder where were his carers and what did they do to prevent the behaviour?

We were always concerned that the main gates of the school were left open, on Monday mornings and Friday afternoons for up to an hour on each occasion, without any staff managing the area. We raised our concerns with the school management, but they told us if the gates were kept shut and everyone had to use the intercom system it would hold up traffic on the main road. Were we therefore left to assume that easy access for vehicles is put before the lives of children that most certainly have no understanding of road safety?

When it was decided to alter Christopher's care package to fifty-two weeks, at the start of the second year, the school Head called us to his office. He was very blunt and told us that under no circumstances were we to talk about this change in front of Christopher. The head teacher also told us that his staff would gradually introduce Christopher to the idea. This did not happen as arranged through the summer holidays and of course when Christopher started the new school year, he proved very difficult to transition to the fifty-two-week idea. Let me explain, the fifty-two-week care system means that the person stays at the school the whole year round but can on occasions come home for weekends or just even an odd day.

When we were out with our son and returning from a dental appointment and accompanied by two carers from the school, we called into McDonald's to give Christopher a treat for being a good boy. The staff that were with us asked about the arrangements for fifty-two-week care. Christopher, also quick to catch on to anything involving himself, had obviously heard what was said and repeated it to someone else at the school. He cannot put sentences together but is very good at Verbatim. Later we were accused of mentioning this in front of our son. So easy for some at schools, particularly the head teacher at this school to blame Mum and Dad and save the necks of his staff. Perhaps it was the staff that lied, and the head teacher would not miss an opportunity like that to get at us.

How about this for co-operation and understanding. We had taken our caravan to the Isle of Wight for a week's break. Unfortunately, our car broke down whilst on the island and we could not get it fixed right away. It was still not ready when we were due to travel home and at that point we did not know if we would be given a courtesy car. We rang the school and warned them that we may be late getting to them and we were told not to worry. However shortly afterwards we received a phone call from the head teacher, who again was very blunt, when he told us that we had to make it on time and that his staff were going home straight after the school day had finished. There was no attempt by this gentleman to offer us any form of help. We did finally manage to rent a car at Southampton and made a mad dash to the school, some thirty to thirty-five miles from the ferry to ensure we arrived on time. Just!

A short time after being refused help, when our car broke down on the Isle of Wight, we attended a behaviour meeting at the school. We requested permission to change a weekend home for Christopher to enable us to take our other son, who also has anxiety and a slow transiting bowel problem to one of the biggest rabbit shows held in this country. Charlie is very enthusiastic about his rabbits, and it helps him to calm down and to spend premium time with his parents. The assistant Residential Manager told us that she could see no problem with our request and so we went ahead with booking and paying for a space for our caravan and all of the entry fees for the rabbits. We then received a letter from the head of the school telling us that it was not possible to change a weekend home for Christopher. When we asked the reason why we were told it was too difficult to get staff and that it was against Christopher's European Human Rights. We have since found this to be incorrect. However, we could not go to the show and had the difficult task of explaining this to our disappointed son, Charlie and of course lost lots of money.

On yet another Wednesday evening we travelled as a family, including our son Charlie, to visit Christopher as we did almost every week. We had become accustomed, and Christopher was used to us meeting and playing with him in the playroom upstairs within the residential block. On this particular evening we were asked to stay in the dining room area and bake a cake with Christopher. As a matter of interest, we noticed later that the playroom was locked and in total darkness and we wondered why? Had Christopher or another child perhaps done something in the room that parents were not allowed to see?

Christopher chose a cake mix and we just about managed to add the ingredients, mix it and hand it to a staff member for baking before the problems started. Christopher asked a staff member for a tomato. He uses these as a sensory aid, cutting them up, sniffing, sometimes licking and eventually throwing them away.

However, his request was ignored. His mother even tried to prompt the staff member by saying loudly enough, "Christopher, let's go in the relaxation room and perhaps you can have a tomato in there". This was also ignored. We did however manage to transition our son to the relaxation room by using a cookie we had brought for him. Once in there he made a request for paper and black pen. This too was ignored until we actually asked on his behalf. Chris then asked for a DVD and chose Chicken Run. The staff member put the DVD into the device but then left, not checking if it was working properly. It wasn't and we had to find the lady and ask her to fix the problem. When this lady returned, I, Christopher's father was writing "A Count Down Note".

When we are going to leave to go home, we usually write on a piece of A4 paper "Mummy and Daddy go home in however many minutes we choose and then do a countdown from 10 or 5 depending on how we feel Christopher is coping. We then cross off the numbers as a timed guide. On this evening there was no paper available in the relaxation room, so the note was written on a small piece of paper taken from my pocket. The note was written and returned to the pocket until needed. We were later to be accused of writing notes about the staff. Anyone making such accusations should first know the facts. In any case had we been writing notes about staff we would have been quite within our rights.

Whilst in the relaxation room we clearly heard Christopher's stomach rumbling very loudly, an indication to us that he was hungry. He asked staff for a packet of crisps and this request was ignored. Christopher's stomach rumbled for a second time. Our son Charlie was worried that his brother was very hungry.

Christopher left the relaxation room and made his way up the stairs and we followed playing a game of hide and seek behind a wall and making various funny noises. Christopher then started kicking and banging various doors and the health and safety notice.

He is an opportunist and we witnessed him trying every door to see if one was unlocked and as it happened, they were secure. Shortly after this a female member of staff went into the office and then back downstairs. At this point Christopher's mother and brother also went back downstairs. Christopher wasted no time in finding out that the office door had been left open and he was in there. What surprised us was that at this time no staff members were with our son, and he was kicking and shouting. Hearing the noise and commotion I entered the office to check what was happening as I was not sure if anyone else was in there. What I found was Christopher taken to the ground by four staff members who had hurried in and Chris was kicking out, pulling one person's hair and biting another... He even managed to grab a pint glass and threw it across the room. Still struggling and having torn down the shower curtain, I asked if staff would like me to go downstairs and ask for another male member of staff to help. The reply was yes and a male at the bottom of the stairs was asked to go up. He asked permission from what was presumed to be a team leader and her answer was an emphatic "No". Incidentally this was the same lady that had left the office open.

Shortly afterwards a lady arrived where we, the family, were stood at the bottom of the stairs waiting to say goodnight to Christopher. We heard her say "Must put my rabbit safe, where's the problem". Is that what our son is "A Problem". We asked what would be best to say goodnight to our son by going up stairs or have him brought down. Not getting any positive answer I, by now getting a little distressed but definitely not loud or shouting, said "Well I am going up to say good night to my son". When I arrived at the top of the stairs Christopher, looking very scared and upset, was huddled in a corner. I bent down and said, "Nite Nite son see you soon". Christopher replied, "Daddy go to playroom with Christopher" and he received a positive reply only to be told that was not possible. Tina then came up gave Chris a kiss and said goodnight. We left the building.

The very next day we received an email from the school head. It was again very blunt and basically, he blamed us for all of the incidents that had happened the previous evening. We were the fault of Christopher's behaviours, and we were now banned from visiting our son in the residential area. If we wanted to visit him in the future, it would be in a room within the main school with two senior members of staff present. This was so hurtful, to be accused, blamed and punished about an evening brought about by bad management of our son's behaviours. If staff had listened to him none of this would have perhaps happened.

The interesting thing being, that although over the last eighteen months there had been eight hundred and thirty incident forms produced and with five or six members of staff involved that not one incident form was produced or passed to us relating to that evening. A complete cover up, obviously it was those terrible parents that were again to blame.

In our opinion the school head should, at the very least, have asked to meet with us and discussed what happened. Instead, he made a very rash decision, one that proved relations between us, and the school had irrevocably broken down. We no longer had any trust for the organisation and no intention of continuing to work with people that have their own opinions and no intention of listening to anyone else or ideas they may have.

Whilst Christopher was at that school, and he spent any time at home, we did not have any major incidents to deal with. We believe that informing Christopher what is happening by means of a schedule, drawn up with him when he arrives home and preparing all activities properly, we are able to control our son and his behaviours. We work as a team and manage Christopher between the two of us. Why we ask can he not be managed safely where there are many more carers and a change of face always available?

I do hope this chapter has not become too long and boring, but I believe it was important for readers to know exactly how difficult life became and mainly because of one belligerent man, who always had to be right and believed he had no need to listen to any other opinions.

You may well be pleased to know that since Christopher left that school the mother of another child was crafty enough to have secret cameras installed. Cameras that proved that staff were deliberately hurting residents, pulling them out of bed by their hair, shutting them in cupboards and banging as loud as possible on the outside and as if that is not enough, it was proved that the carers were encouraging the residents to punch themselves. Could this have happened to our son? We will never know. Thank God, the courts ordered the residential part of that establishment to be closed down.

Just a last word. Why there were pint glasses available for Chris to throw. Apparently, some of the staff used the staff room to hold parties and consume alcohol. The thought comes to mind as to whether the head knew of these parties or, perhaps he was sometimes present.

CHAPTER 8

Pupil Premium

I don't know how many of you might remember something the UK government have given to many special needs children, called Pupil Premium. I believe it still exists and I have given you a link at the end of the chapter so you can easily check it out. If the link does not work for you, just use good old Google and type in Pupil Premium, that's how I checked it out. It was designed to help those children that needed something extra, maybe an I Pad or something similar, maybe something to help a group of children.

After making enquiries, we were informed that Christopher was entitled to Pupil Premium and as parents thought it would be most useful if our son had an I Pad equipped with the correct software to help with his communication, understanding and comprehension and frustration because others cannot always understand what he wants. Pupil Premium does not seem to be something that is openly advertised, perhaps because the money is paid to local councils, and it is up to them who actually receives it. Maybe, it is used for other things within the local authority's budget, but it should surely be kept for the use it was meant to be for.

We took advice from parents of another autistic child who regularly uses an I Pad, also purchased with Pupil Premium, who had found that it had helped their child enormously with communication and frustration. They were kind enough to give us a demonstration of the I Pad that was equipped with a Pecs programme called Sonoflex. I Pads are used frequently by many children that have communication problems, for instance for something as simple as asking for an orange or maybe a cup of tea. Things that we take for granted but that so many on the spectrum cannot do.

We made the request to Christopher's School in Dorset but were told by the head teacher that Christopher was not entitled to Pupil Premium. We were unhappy with this answer and so I did no more that wrote to the education minister at the time, a certain ROH Michael Gove MP. Little did I think my letter would get through or even answered. Wow, how wrong can you be. It was about a week later when I received a phone call from a private number. Quite often I don't bother answering these calls but thank goodness on that particular day I did. I recognised the voice at the end of the phone but could not put a name to it, that said "Is that Mr Parker"? Once I had confirmed I was indeed Charles Parker, the voice continued. "Good afternoon, Mr Parker, my name is Michael Gove, minister for Education. I have got your letter and I am so pleased to hear from you. Too many schools and local authorities are using the Pupil Premium for the wrong reasons. I shall be dealing with this matter for you very shortly and you will be receiving notice that your son's money will be available to use soon. Do get back to me if you have any other trouble. Thank you for your time and goodbye for now."

Astonished, is not the word. Thank you, Mr Gove, who says it's not worth contacting these people.

Within the next few days, I received a letter from the school head, eating his words, making out he had made a genuine error. I found out that not only was my son eligible for pupil premium, but it was also confirmed that nearly every child in the school was now eligible. It was paid according to the severity of the disability and could be worth as much as nine hundred to one thousand pounds to Christopher, each year, for the next three or four years. As his parents we were very grateful. We were able to get some very useful equipment for Chris including a digital camera, his I Pad and a laptop as he moved further through his educational journey.

It seemed to take a very long time for the I Pad, the first item we ordered, to arrive but finally we were told it had and that Christopher was being gradually introduced to it. We had ordered a safety case and requested software including the special Pecs programme on it. The case, Griffin being the best, is all important, without it I don't think the I Pad would have lasted five minutes.

Several more weeks followed, and we were under the impression that our son was making progress with the I Pad. The idea was for him to get used to it in the educational setting then progress to using it in the residential setting and at home. We were then invited to a parents evening where we met Christopher's second year teacher.

When we raised the subject of the I Pad we were amazed. He produced it and the safety case, both still wrapped up and clearly not used. We had been told a pack of lies. Was this the teacher at fault or that of the man who thought he was God over the school.

We made it known that we were not happy and hoped that Christopher would soon be taught how to use the I Pad to his benefit. Still trying to win, or beat us, we received another rather blunt letter from the head teacher, the man on high, who thought he was untouchable, telling us that Christopher was not entitled to Pupil premium. That anything he was given, would not move with him if he changed schools. (This was contrary to what we were told by friends with children at other schools. We were also told Chris would not be allowed to bring the I Pad home.

Well Mr Head Teacher, here just for you and my readers of course are the facts. The I Pad and many other useful bits of equipment were bought for Christopher. He took all of that with him when he moved to another school, which as you have probably guessed was inevitable. Now having left school Chris has everything still with him. Sorry you didn't get your own way on that one Sir. Very sorry, if between us, the ROH Michael Gove and me, put an end to your "School Roof Fund". Apparently, there are many schools throughout England that have used the Pupil Premium Fund for the wrong reasons denying many children of what they are rightfully entitled to each year.

If it's of any help, I have at the time of writing used Google to find out the following for my readers and the parents with children in need. Here's what I have just read and hope it is a help to many.

"Children can be eligible for the pupil premium for a variety of reasons. These include their family circumstances, such as their income or occupations, and whether or not they are in care. If a child is eligible, a school will receive the necessary amount of funding for each child per school year."

One then has to hope for honesty from the school and that they do not have a school roof fund in place. If you have any doubts, contact your Member of Parliament and ask for their help. Far better to do that than contact the local council as some of them have also been known to divert Pupil Premium funds, as I said earlier.

To help any of you that might like to know more about Pupil Premium, here are some links that may be useful, why not check them out.

The parent's guide to the pupil premium | TheSchoolRun

https://www.theschoolrun.com/parents-guide-pupil-premium

Or simply Google Pupil Premium where you will find lots of information.

CHAPTER 9

Christopher Speaks

In some of the chapters there has been so much to write that I thought it might be a good idea to add in one or two extra chapters, giving me the chance to tell you about some stand out moments.

The special moments in this chapter all happened at the school he attended in Dorset and I warn you in advance that many are far from positive. Remember I mentioned earlier that Chris, and indeed most people that struggle to speak, do in fact talk through their behaviours.

The moments I am going to share with you right now are not all about my son's behaviours, but many are of course. Others are about things that happened or things that were done by staff at the school and for the life of me I have never worked out why.

Try to work this one out. What was Christopher trying to tell his teacher when he donkey kicked the interactive White Board in the classroom, breaking it and causing around eight hundred pounds worth of damage. I never got to the bottom of this one as the teacher was unable to tell Tina and I what the antecedent to the incident had been. So important if you want to untangle the message you must know the why? One thought, could he have got fed up with the restraints placed upon him?

On another occasion Chris broke the window in his bedroom. Again no one knew what caused him to do it, but I would hazard a guess it was because he wanted to go outside and was prevented from doing so for one reason or another. The response from the head teacher was to have the window securely boarded up and that worried me. I approached the head and asked firstly in a polite manner if what he had done was legal and whether it was safe. "Of course," was his reply, "I know what I am doing and in any case, I have spoken to the fire brigade". I was not at all sure he was right on either of his answers, but he always had to be right.

I put it to him that should there be a fire right outside of Chrissy's bedroom door that he could be trapped. He certainly couldn't get out through the window. Was this within fire regulation, I asked. It was very worrying, and we kept reminding the school, in writing, that they would be held fully responsible if anything were to go wrong, or our son was injured or worse.

One day, Christopher trashed much of his bedroom and of course it was his fault and according to the head teacher our fault as parents. As luck would have it, we were at the school later that day, visiting and we were told about our son's handy work and asked to take a look. On entering the bedroom, it was immediately obvious how Christopher had dug chunks out of the wall. Laying on the bed was a screwdriver, left by someone that had been working in the room earlier that day. It was an open invitation to our son; could you blame him if he was bored? Even when the screwdriver was pointed out to the guy who knew it all, it was still our son's fault. His words, "He should know better". Did this man know anything about autism? I ask you; I think any normal kid would find it hard if they came across a screwdriver not to experiment with it.

To our son, it was magic, he had always liked digging away at the plaster in his bedroom at home when he was much younger but then it was with his fingernails, here he had it made. The only answer we had back home was to have the room converted to a fully padded, air-conditioned room, at a total cost if my memory serves me well of between seven and eight thousand pounds. I think we should all thank God that Christopher did not poke the screwdriver into any of the electrical sockets, the ones that were supposed to have been covered for safety reasons. Why didn't Mr Know All listen to anyone else?

One of Christopher's loves was to be outside and, on a trampoline, and if his carers refused him that privilege, he would take matters into his own hands and look for an opportunity to escape through an open window. I remember on one occasion he escaped, and the carers were doing such a good job that they didn't even know he was missing. We often found things like this out from another carer that wanted to score some extra Brownie points. They would tell us what had happened, perhaps hoping to fish for any answers or information we might let slip.

Needless to say, we were always very careful what we shared but made sure we always had an open ear. It may well be that the good advice my dear old dad had given me many years earlier was paying off. "Son", he said, "You have two ears and one mouth, make sure you always use them in that proportion." Thank you, Dad. I have always done my best to live up to that sound advice but sometimes it has become very difficult.

Christopher has always loved writing and drawing. He was never that fussy what he used but when outside in the playground he preferred chalk. Leave our son with a handful of chalk and he was happy, he would spend endless hours writing away. Mind carers had been warned to look out for any words that were not eligible for the English dictionary. You would know when Chris had used any of these as he would laugh and say, "What have you done".

One of the other things that we warned carers about, when Chris first arrived on the scene was his ability the throw stones, long, high and certainly hard. However, we were there one evening, when the carer was busy texting on his phone and totally oblivious as to what our son was up to. Chris was writing one minute, finding a lovely big stone the next and heaving it at one of the windows. I surely don't have to tell you the result, perhaps enough just to say that Chris had the broadest of smiles on his innocent little face and that bold statement, "What have you done"? Ten points to Chris on that one.

Fairly close to the school was a garden centre. Not that it's important but I always remember the name, Ploughman's, the same name as a very good friend of mine that I had known for years. A smashing chap, always very honest and outspoken and someone that always reassured us that whilst at his church he would lead prayers for Chris and us as a family. I Will never forget you, Malcolm.

Now back to the garden centre. At Christmas they always did something special for the public and indeed for many of the local schools. They had a miniature railway going all around the garden centre perimeter and even at my age I enjoyed it.

They had times available for those with special needs. It gave Chris and others like him, a chance to meet with Father Christmas. Oh, it was so funny, and the staff were so helpful. We explained that Chris did not understand about waiting in queues and they were on the ball right away. Normally there may be as many as twenty on the train but so that Christopher did not get worked up, they did a ride with just our family on board. It was wonderful and at the end when Father Christmas gave both of our sons a present Chris tried to say thank you by biting the bearded wonder.

After the visit it was straight home for the Christmas holidays, two weeks where we would have to be very much alert but also hope we could be blessed with a somewhat peaceful time for the sake of our other son Charlie. This would actually be the last Christmas, although we did not know it at the time that Christopher would join us at home for the festivities. Sad, I know, but with behaviours worsening it was a case of necessity and for the safety of us all.

Whilst in the Christmas mood, let me tell you about something that made both Tina and I very happy. The day that we were at the school to bear witness to our son playing the part of an angel in the school's production of the Nativity. Unbelievable, that for a young man that could be so difficult and yet he had been able to wear the wings his mum had made for him, stand on the stage with others and make us, mum and dad, feel immensely proud. That was to say the least, a very special moment, that we will never forget.

One of the advantages for Chris at this school was that he did not have to leave the school site for his overnight ritual, it was all there, within walking distance. Probably, not so easy for staff if they were not paying attention, you know on their phones, because Chris learnt to know every inch of the school site, all the short cuts and because of that led a few of the staff a right merry dance when he was in the mood.

Other places that Chris used to be taken and have fun included some dry slopes at a place called Two River Meet, a massive country park, called Moors Valley and a local Trampoline club, although one day when coming out of the latter the carers were again not doing their job properly. They failed to link arms with Chris and seeing a little old lady not far in front he proceeded to slap her on the back and deliver her to the floor. I believe the matter was reported to the police but cooled down by an apology and a beautiful bunch of flowers. Christopher's response, "Say sorry to the lady". He knew he had done wrong and was apologetic immediately. Unfortunately, that is autism.

At every school Christopher has attended his risk assessments have never changed, in that they state he must have a minimum of two carers when in the community. When Chris slapped that lady, one must ask, what were the carers doing at the time? Were they close enough to stop it happening? Were they alert enough? Were they again paying more attention to their mobile phones?

Remember, I have said it before, Chris, when he has a behavioural issue, he is talking to us. So, what was he trying to say when he hit out at that lady. It's a difficult one and we may never work it out, but he was definitely trying to tell his carers something. Maybe he knew they were not doing their job properly. Maybe he felt like hitting one of the carers but saw the lady a much easier target.

Let us look more deeply into this particular attack. We know that Chris has witnessed carers at the Dorset school doing some terrible things that they shouldn't. Things that maybe Chris has at times, had to personally endure whilst there and he wanted to get his own back.

I may not be anywhere near the truth but knowing why the residential unit at that school was closed down, I may not be too far from it either.

Still today we firmly believe that some of what Christopher did at that school and continues to tell us from statements he still makes, he has been badly affected by his time there. I would go as far as to say he and perhaps others at that school were psychologically scarred. I believe our son is still scarred and although the school we found him after this tortuous time worked religiously for five years to help repair the trauma, some of it still remains. Not to let too much out of the bag about his future, I will just say that what I still have to write and bring to you will send shivers down your spine.

Boy, there are some people in the caring industry that are brilliant and then there are others that are nothing short of useless and some I would go as far as saying evil. Can you wonder at it that young people like our son choose to use behaviours, many of which we do not approve of, as their way of conversing with us. Personally, I am glad that they do it. How else would we be given any clues that all is not well?

Charles Parker

CHAPTER 10

The End and New Beginning

What a mistake we had made! We had been fooled by the bright shiny paint and the thought of a swimming pool but in all honesty looking back we must ask ourselves what else did they offer Christopher?

History, a very brave parent and the courts have of course proved that they, the management and some of the staff at the Dorset establishment let so many young people down. The way we were spoken to on some occasions was nothing short of disgusting. The way we were blamed at many of the behaviour meetings for what our son did. It was always what we did at home that caused the behaviours at school. That is until, as I mentioned previously, the educational psychologist had heard enough and stuck up for us. Fortunately, that gentleman came to our home for meetings very often and saw first-hand how we looked after our children, including when Chris was at home on some occasions.

Some may say they and their children, didn't get treated too badly at that school but to those people I would ask whether or not they had the courage to challenge the management, to ask the questions that you know would probably be met with conflict. Were you a parent, that was happy your child was basically in the care of the school and that you could carry on living your life to the full. To be honest, I can understand it if a parent was like that. It is not easy, battling away to get what your child needs particularly coming up against management like those that were in charge at this school. God was it hard work!

I think it very much depends what sort of person you are and what exactly you are prepared to accept. Tina and I have always only wanted the best for Christopher, and we were not prepared to accept that people with dictatorial attitudes have their own way all of the time when it came to looking after our child. Not when we knew full well that the way our son was being looked after was not good enough, nowhere near good enough in the second year.

The easy answer to any problem is to back down, take the yes sir no sir approach but is that really fair on your child, particularly a child for whom you are its voice. When you entrust your child to any establishment you must remain very much on the ball, so to speak. No one likes to constantly mistrust anyone but there are times you must accept the true responsibility that comes with being a mother and father. I, for sure have no plans to go into any meeting that involves the future of my son, or any relative come to that and aim to be the most popular person around. If you're like that then understand that you will become easy to push around.

Well, here we were, in a situation where we thought Chris would be staying at school for the summer holidays but instead, we had to look after him for all of that time, without, it would seem any help at all. At the same time, we had to find a new school in time for the autumn term. That for sure, would take hard work and one hell of a lot of luck. Where could we possibly start? We knew from the outset of our search this time that there would not be an abundance of schools within Hampshire, that could meet our son's needs. Would this mean that we may have to start looking much further afield, maybe that would mean that we too had to up sticks to be closer to Chris.

If that's what was needed, we were prepared to do just that. Not being a youngster, I remember the words of the great Doris Day, Que Sera Sera (Whatever will be will be) Anything, anytime for our children. That has been and will always remain mine and my wife's belief and philosophy.

After finding three schools in the past, all-in affect that had failed our son, we started to wonder whether this was our fault, something we were doing. Were we expecting too much? In hindsight I personally don't think so. No child or parent should be dealt second best. We must not lower our expectant standards; we must raise them until we find the very best. One theory we had and still is that many schools and homes in the care industry, look for the cheapest options. They do not provide enough or proper training for their staff. Many, perhaps through no fault of their own, are forced to take on staff from agencies. That could mean they are sent someone that the day before may have been working at a burger bar. That in fact is not a guess. One young lady at the Dorset school told us one evening that it was her first day in care and that the day before she had in fact been serving burgers to the public. What time did she have for any proper training?

Lady Luck? Thank you! We just happened to be doing a bit of surfing from home when something hit out at us. We saw a mention of Hill House School.

You remember the school we rejected in an instant; rejected at first sight, all because we had been blinded by the bright fresh paintwork in Dorset. How wrong can you be. How many times must we be told, how many times must we stop and think to never ever judge a book by its cover. Finally, I think we had learnt our lesson.

We read how, in the two years that our son had been at Dorset, that Hill House School had been improved beyond recognition and even more work was planned. What did we have to lose? Picking up the phone and dialling the number I felt almost embarrassed. Here was I, about to ask about vacancies at a school my wife and I had rated second best. It's that judging a book by its cover syndrome, come back to bite us again.

Nevertheless, I thought, they will not know we had looked at the school before, we don't need to feel guilty or embarrassed. A lovely lady answered the phone and asked us various questions at the end of which we had two very big, and very important questions for her:.

Do you have any vacancies for a fifteen-year-old?

Can we visit and view the school?

Oddly, the lady answered the second question first saying yes of course we could look around the school and she made us an appointment there and then.

With regard to having a vacancy, that was a little more complicated. Silly me, I should have realised that before anyone could say yes to Christopher, they would first need to meet us, meet our son and most importantly complete an assessment. Then it would be a case of getting funding approved. None of this was straight forward but we were encouraged by what we had been told and were very excited about our planned visit.

We had decided, when we visited Hill House that we would be very open and honest about what had happened at the last school and indeed at Christopher's previous schools. The big day arrived; we drove through the New Forest and eventually found the school tucked away in a quiet and beautiful surrounding. Wow, we read on the internet that remedial work had been done and we were flabbergasted to see the change. A building that had once housed a private boy's school, taken over by the Cambian Group had suddenly started to look like a school that with some imagination one could truly envisage would become the envy of many.

We were met by a lady who introduced herself as the school secretary and she in turn took us through to the head teacher's study. However, having been introduced we were informed by the head teacher that she was in fact The Acting Head Teacher. She explained that the school was still in the process of making many improvements, one being that the previous head had left or been relieved of her duties and that another had been chosen but was unable to start immediately.

The person we spoke to was amazing, made you feel very welcome and gave you the feeling that the school, with lots of its work completed would be a brilliant fit for our son. We wanted it to happen, so it was now down to the staff to carry out their assessments and to see if there was an appropriate vacancy for Christopher. Also of course we would need the agreement of the Southampton Local Authority agreeing to pay what would be more than Chris's education had ever been. Quite a bit more actually, just over a quarter of a million a year.

So, there was nothing more we could do on that score for the time being, not until we heard when the school wanted to meet Christopher.

In the meantime we had a minimum of six weeks to look after Christopher, certainly until we got an assurance from Hill House. Or find another school if they felt they couldn't educate and look after our son for at least the next four years.

During that particular period, we were both extremely anxious. Waiting and hoping for the right answer. Imagine, what would we do if Hill House said no, what time was there to find another appropriate placement?

With Chris now home for several weeks it meant that he expected his normal home time ritual of getting up early, going out every morning in the car, returning home via the chippy for his batty sausage and chips and then once fully charged to go back out in the car for the afternoon. A weekend, yes possible, but for weeks on end it would be very tiring. Milage and fuel were two things that quickly mounted as well, and at that time the cost was down to us.

After about a week or so and quite out of the blue, we received a phone call from a private number. Should we answer or not? Normally we would not because most of the time it was someone trying to sell you something. Then I thought, it could be Hill House school trying to fix a time to complete their assessment, so I answered. Hello, said a voice that I didn't recognise, is that Mr Parker. I confirmed it was me on the phone and was then truly blown away from what came next. Mr Parker the lady said, as she introduced herself. I have been put in temporary charge of Social Services in Southampton and it has reached my ear that you have a problem. I believe you have your son, Christopher home for the whole of the holidays and it has been whispered that you are spending many hours taking him out every day in the car. Is that correct?

I quickly explained that it was indeed correct and what made it more difficult was that we had no help, no respite and yes, that it was extremely exhausting both for me and my dear wife.

Well, I want to help you, the lady replied. She had been told just how very difficult it was to care for Christopher. Still to this day, I am none the wiser who sent this particular angel to our door, but her intervention was so much appreciated. She told me that she intended to put some special carers in place every day, seven days a week, from eight in the morning to ten o'clock at night. Wow, some shift, but some welcome relief, let me tell you. Our angel said she would make a few calls and be back to us as soon as possible.

She wasted no time; she called us back that very same day and confirmed the help would start the next day. She informed us she had contracted Thornbury Nursing to help look after Chris every day until a school was sorted and our son started there.

Thornbury Nursing, "The Tops"! All of those that came to us were grade five mental health nurses, travelling from all parts of the country, including as far afield as South and North Wales, Wolverhampton and goodness knows where else. One guy, travelled from Gloucester, and appeared to be on the schedule almost every day. His name was Simon, and he was such an understanding person. He and Christopher had an almost immediate understanding of each other, a clear respect that showed through.

Simon and another carer would arrive just before eight, sometimes before I got back home with Christopher from the early morning jaunt around the New Forest, or wherever had taken my son's fancy that day. Off they would go, and we would then not see Christopher until lunch time, unless the carers decided to feed Chris whilst out, which gradually would break the habit of the chippy.

Those Thornbury guys, men and women, were brilliant. It seemed that whatever Chris came up with in terms of behaviours they had the answer. We learned so much from them. I am not trying to say that before Thornbury turned up that we knew nothing, of course that's not the case. We made it our mission if you like, to be constantly learning, studying, reading, to develop a far better understanding of autism and how we might be able to improve Christopher's life and ours alike.

No one can ever know it all and I am a very firm believer that the way to learn more about mental health is to work with it or alongside it in your own home or family. It's a bit like learning to drive without sitting in the driving seat, trying to learn to knit without needles and some wool. I think you get my meaning.

It's also very important to know when to ask for support, to call in the cavalry. That is not a weakness, it can make everything so much better if you are prepared to learn more yourself. Understanding this is so important. Never put yourself down, always think positively. Asking for help and support does not make you less of a person. Having Thornbury gave us so much, even allowed us to catch up on some sleep in the afternoon if we needed it.

It allowed us to spend some time with our other son Charlie and to have an hour or two some days just being ourselves and being there for one another. God bless Thornbury. God Bless that Angel from Social Services.

Never before had we had what amounted to a voluntary input from our local authority. On the contrary we had usually been met by a wall of opposition. Indeed, that Angel, in our lives for such a short time was a one off within the system and no one since has ever been so helpful.

Arguments and battles recommenced as soon as she left and have continued still to this day. It seems to me that most of those that take up jobs within the local authority are more intent on ruling the roost, rather than working towards an outcome that brings about improvement for the person and their immediate family. In fact, I remember someone saying to me when Chris was at school, "You think you have problems now, just wait until your son moves into adult care."

How relieved were we when we heard that two ladies from Hill House, Amanda and Adina would be coming to our home to meet with us and of course more importantly to meet Christopher. Another lady, the deputy head at Hill House, Carmen had been doing her homework at Christopher's previous school and we later learnt how disgusted she was with the attitude of that establishment.

The big day arrived, it was Adina and Amanda at our front door, boy were we nervous. We needn't have been because as soon as they came into our home, they made us feel so at ease. Questions and answers were free flowing, and Christopher was on top form. There appeared to be an almost instant bond between Chris and Adina, who we learnt soon after that meeting at home would be our sons first teacher at Hill House. You have guessed now no doubt that

Christopher had been accepted as a fifty-two-week border at the school and that he would start in September 2013.

I mentioned a bond between Chris and Adina. That bond was cemented together at our home on the morning they met, when Christopher gave his teacher a great big hug. I think and know for sure that Adina was truly moved by this, we prayed that what had been started in such a positive manner would be continued.

Once it was confirmed that Chris was moving into Hill House School Tina wasted no time in producing a social story for him in the form of a picture story. A picture of Hill House with numbers on it making the countdown to what would we hoped would be a wonderful future. Full marks to Tina, the countdown house or pictorial social story worked amazingly well. Every morning Chris would come downstairs and his very first job, without any prompting most days, was to cross off the next number, and after crossing out the number he would announce the number of sleeps left till he started his new school. Chris never has and I don't suppose ever will count time in days. Sleeps, that is his word, he's happy with it and why should we try to change it.

During the time leading up to the start date we drove Christopher around the area of the forest where Hill House was in Boldre, near Lymington and he was made welcome for brief visits to the school, getting used to his room, which was in the "Oaks". All of the areas of the school were named after trees. Where the Oaks was positioned could not have been better because the lounge area of that house lead directly on to the school playground. Every time we took Chris he appeared to gain in confidence and seemed to be less nervous.

Everyone we met was so friendly and yet kept a professional side that made us feel confident that finally this school would be the right one. Could this be the first school that our son had attended that was not just a one-year wonder and second year flop. Time would tell.

Top: *Celebrating his 15th birthday.*

Bottom: *a fantastic picture of our beautiful young man.*

Top*: Studying at Hill House.*

Bottom*: Christmas
2013 with Dad at Hill
House School.*

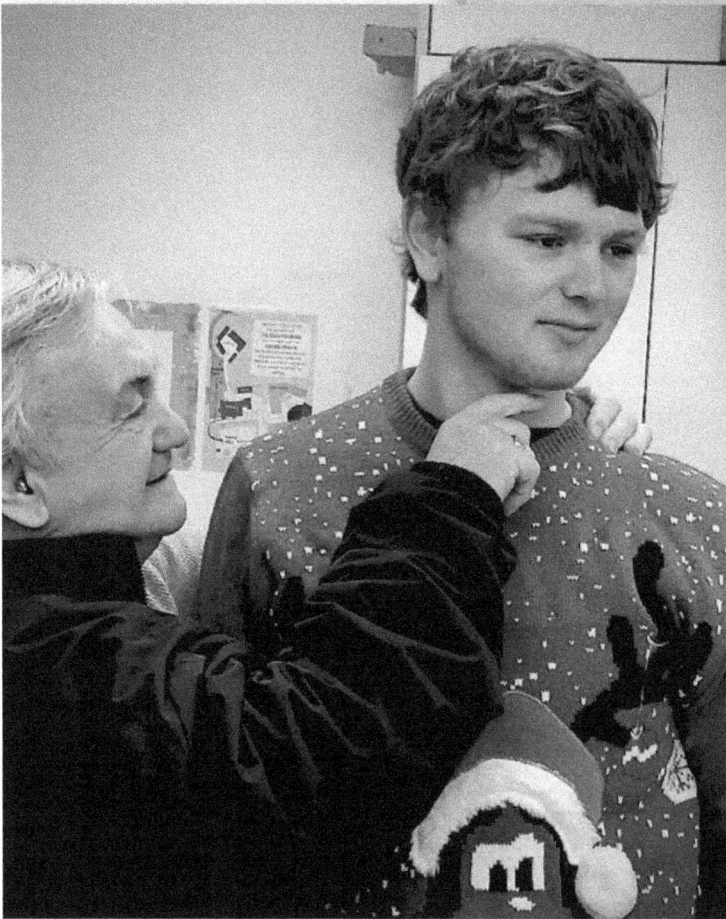

CHAPTER 11

A New School, A New Chapter

Finally, with the last piece of the puzzle in place as Southampton Local Authority agreed to fund Christopher as a 52-week border at Hill House. With everything in place, it was just a case of waiting for the big day. Hill House would not come cheap, Chris was to be looked after by two carers, a 2-1 system whilst on the school site and more if required when he went out on trips.

September 2013, the day had arrived, we were to take Chris to Hill House for his official start. Whether Chris felt differently to going to this new school, we are not sure but there wasn't any bad behaviour as we took him to the car and drove to the New Forest.

We were met on arrival by Adina, Christopher's new teacher, that I introduced you to briefly in the last chapter. Chris was quite happy to go with Adina and we were to get our first opportunity to meet with the school's new Head Teacher.

"Good morning Charles, Good morning Tina, I am Kate Landells and will be responsible for looking after your son together with all the other children that we have here". That beaming smile said so much, it put us at ease and after talking for a while with Kate, we realised that this school was definitely different to any other Christopher had been part of. Kate emphasised that everyone involved at the school, including us as parents were part of a team. A team that would always be encouraged to pull together and if there were any problems at all, they were to be aired without delay, sorted out and then move on. What an amazing start, what a wonderful attitude.

Kate promised that a member of staff would keep us updated later that day and before we left the school introduced us to one of the persons that was a joint manager of the Oaks, where Christopher would sleep. Martyn, what a lovely man, whilst we understood the other person on the second shift was a lady named Amanda. It was a really big ask for Chris to settle in quickly but because his teacher made him feel wanted and the staff at the Oaks were so warm towards everyone it all got off to a wonderful start.

Kate gave us permission to use her first name and in fact said she much preferred it as it created a far better atmosphere throughout the school, there was no doubt a definite air of friendliness. She did not seem in any hurry for us to leave, Chris had gone to his class with Adina and Kate used the time to find out more about Christopher and ourselves. It also gave us so much confidence, both in Kate and the school. Eventually we left for home and eagerly awaited an update later. That phone call arrived in the early evening from Martyn and he assured us that Chris was accepting both the school and the Oaks very well. How wonderful to think that finally we may have found a placement that would prove right for our son and where staff were prepared to work with you, to listen to any advice you could offer and in turn make things better all round.

We had another update on the second day, Tuesday, again very positive and looked forward to our first visit on Wednesday evening. We continued the same visiting arrangements that we had done at previous schools, picking Chris up, driving him out to Mac Donald's, with a bit of a drive around the forest then back to Hill House. When we arrived back, we were invited to stay for a while and we noticed something so different at this school. Christopher, like many others was looked after on a two to one basis, yet we could only see one carer with Chris and some of the others that were out in the playground.

I could not resist asking, why does Chris not have two carers? Oh, he does, Amanda answered, she was on the evening shift. She continued to explain that one carer would always work quite closely, within touching distance, with our son whilst the other was in the shadow, as she explained it, ready to jump in if needed. This way, it did not over crowd Chris, he felt he had freedom but of course he also had all the care he required. That was so good to hear. The staff at Hill House had really thought this through and you could see everyone out in the playground looked happy and content.

Everything went so well at Hill House, as Christopher settled in and made great progress through his first year. The whole atmosphere was different to anything Chris or we had experienced at any other of his schools. That's not to say that everything went Hunky Dory all of the time, of course there were moments when our son flipped, maybe wanted his own way and was encouraged to do things differently.

Chris soon found out where Kate's office was within the building and that he could look in her window. One evening Kate was working late, as she often did and I guess Chris wanted to attract her attention. He would often tap on her window and Kate would at the very least give a little wave. This particular evening Kate was busy and fully concentrated on her work, but our son was not going to be denied making contact. He hit his elbow against the window, breaking it and in turn cutting himself. Apparently, all the other windows were toughened glass, except this tiny little one. Trust Chris to find that very small one that wasn't. With suspected glass in the wound, it was a trip to the nearest hospital, a small local place just a few miles away in Lymington. Now in the past hospital trips were normally very difficult, very confrontational in fact but apparently Christopher on this occasion was brilliantly well behaved. I truly believe, having learnt so much about Hill House over the years, that Chris's behaviour on that day was because of the way he was handled by the staff from such a fine school. So, no major worries, wound cleaned up, it was back to Hill House where our son enjoyed the rest of his evening as if nothing had happened.

Kate, the head teacher was very special. She would surprise the whole school with treats some days. On a couple of occasions, I heard that Kate had gone to a local farm on a Sunday, collected enough Strawberries, for staff and residents and then going into the school made sure everyone had their fair share. How thoughtful and kind is that? A Special Lady – SIMPLY THE BEST. That phrase, who does that remind you of?

There were so many special people at Hill House. Special for different reasons. Special because they helped our son achieve so much, in so many different fields.

One lady, Gaynor, certainly deserves special mention. She became so close to Chris whilst he was at Hill House. She had this amazing way of counting up to five when Chris chose to turn a blind ear to her requests. Without doubt the affinity between our son and Gaynor was something one would have to go such a long way to see again. When Gaynor heard that it was time for Chris to leave Hill House, she was one of the first to shed tears. She asked if we would be happy to have a life size cardboard cut-out of Chris so that she could keep the real thing. In some ways, we too wish Chris could have stayed on, at a place he was so happy and maybe have been found a little job there, perhaps an apprentice gardener.

Let me tell you about one more staff member that was a "stand out." It was Carmen, during her assessment, that realised what Chris had been missing out on and what he had to offer to Hill House. Thank God that lady was very perceptive and had a very forward-thinking mind. It was such a shame when she decided to move to another school but with opportunity of promotion together with her amazing skills, no one had the right to deny her.

As I continue to share some of the amazing stories of Christopher at Hill House, I will tell you about others that were very special to Chris and extremely special to the school for the efforts they put in.

In Christopher's early weeks at Hill House, it was felt best if he came home at weekends. We would take a nice relaxing drive out through the forest on a Friday afternoon to pick up Christopher and take him home. One of the massive differences we noticed was that no one was in a hurry, things were done at Christophers pace, he was the one that mattered. On one particular Friday Christopher was having a bit of a meltdown. Did it matter to the staff how long it took to calm him down? Not at all, in fact I was waiting over an hour but when Chris eventually was ready to travel home, he was very calm. It was so important, to be patient and just give him time.

Compare that to his last school. We were told by the head teacher that we must be at the school on time, that as soon as the school finished staff would be going home and that it was not their duty to hang around caring for any of the children. We witnessed appalling handling of our son on many Fridays but none worse than one particular week, when he had donkey kicked the electronic wipe clean board.   Six male staff picked Christopher up, carried him to my car and bundled him in the back. Is it no wonder that every Monday morning, knowing where he was again heading that our son did not want to get dressed, get in the car and return to this terrible school.

Fortunately, whenever Christopher had been home from Hill House for a couple of days, he was not at all reluctant to go back. Both Tina and I had realised from this that our son was settled, that we had found the right school and that he was being treated with the upmost respect.

Let me make one more comparison between his last school and Hill House and I promise I will not mention them together on the same page again. It may seem something, that in your mind is not massive but believe me it was something that mattered so much. At the last place, staff looking after Christopher were constantly seen on their personal mobile phones, texting so much of the time. At Hill House staff were forbidden to use their phones whilst on duty and there would be serious consequences if they were caught. Only managers were allowed to make calls, using the school phone given to them for that specific purpose. All staff had to leave their personal phones in their locker, no excuses accepted.

The reason I mention this is because many of the incidents that happened in Dorset, happened because the staff were in another world, they certainly were not paying attention to our son. Had they been there would have been far less broken windows, that is for sure.

At Hill House it was a policy of all working together as a team, including the parents, to help Christopher gradually improve on each of the subjects he studied. We learnt that patience was paramount to our son moving forward, and at Hill House there was an abundance of patience and understanding, flowing through the whole school as freely as a river.

By the time Christopher's next birthday came around, November, he had been at Hill House for about three months. He had settled in and started to get back to being the cheeky fella with a smashing smile that we had known before his previous school had ruined it all. We have always made a fuss about all family birthdays, and we could not believe how staff helped to make his first at Hill House extra special. We were allowed to use the school hall and many of the other residents along with staff attended. The sound of disco music, along with images of Chris projected on the walls completed several fantastic birthdays in his time at Hill House.

Another asset that Chris had was a willingness to help anyone. Helping the old boy, Bill who was well in his seventies but still did the gardening. Chris could often be seen pushing the wheelbarrow around for him, raking up leaves and sweeping up, all things that Christopher loved. He was also able to turn his hand to helping in the school office, using the photocopy machine was one job that he absolutely loved to do.

Another thing that Christopher was always encouraged to do whilst at Hill House School was go for plenty of long walks and he had no objection. The local surroundings were made for walking. Carers had to be especially careful on some roads as there were no pavements, but with two of them out with Chris they kept a close eye and a tight arm where they felt it necessary. Chris has always loved walking and to this day insists on having a walk after we have taken him for his regular treat at MacDonalds.

Without doubt the biggest difference between previous schools, particularly the last one and that of Hill House is summed up in one very important word. *RESPECT.* At Hill House respect was a conditional requirement and it was seen in abundance. It was, for the first time, in many a day, amazing how everyone at Hill House respected everyone else, whether it be parents, fellow staff, residents or just an occasional visitor. All were shown respect and that had a reciprocal affect throughout the whole establishment.

What's more, is that we personally felt that respect and had every confidence that, with that in mind, our son was on to a winner, a future he could enjoy and make serious progress. Having lost trust and confidence, having been put through the wringer by many others before, we felt the time had arrived where we genuinely were feeling the warmth from the arms of Hill House stretch out, hug us and welcome us onboard. Not just Christopher but the whole family.

CHAPTER 12

Special Days and Events at Hill House

During the five happy years Christopher had at Hill House, there was never a dull moment. Kate and her wonderful staff arranged many great days at the school.

Different types of music from string quartets to one I remember well and knew that Chris particularly enjoyed was a steel band. Wow! They were brilliant. More than just entertaining, all of the groups of musicians had that special something that appeared to send everyone, including staff, pupils and any parents that might have heard a whisper that they were coming, into a complete state of relaxation.

One of the days we were proud to help with was introducing the children to our rabbits. At the time we bred and showed rabbits to a high show standard and taking some of them into the school for a morning gave many of the kids an opportunity to get close up, to feed them with some tip bits and get to feel their beautiful coats.

I remember the very first time we took the bunnies to Hill House, with reluctance at first from most of the children, to get too close. It was new to them and they didn't want to get near them. With lots of patience and with Chris showing his school mates there was no need to be afraid, for he had been encouraged when at home to feed and smooth them, gradually almost all of the pupils found the courage to move much closer and find out what it was like to smooth these beautiful bunnies.

At home we all found grooming the rabbits very therapeutic. I am convinced that many of the children at Hill House were helped by the contact. What makes me think that? The fact that quite a few of them came back to the rabbits more than once, some several times, they were building their own confidence and starting to feel safe. Having three different breeds meant there were three different types of feel to the coats and I truly believe some of Christopher's autistic friends recognised that.

We were able to take three different breeds each time we visited. Tina bred Netherland Dwarfs, tiny little rabbits with a maximum weight of two and a half pounds, Charlie bred and showed Himalayan Rex, their coats like velvet and my breed was English Lops. They were very large bunnies with great big, long ears. From ear tip to ear tip many of them measured twenty-nine inches, with a width of six inches. These were the ones that perhaps made the children most wary but, in all honesty, they were gentle giants. Incidentally, it is with much pleasure that I am able to say that all three of us, at different times, had achieved best in show with our breeds.

Spending a few hours at the school, with the rabbits and being able to see how they helped the children was as I have already said very therapeutic for us as well as the children. I think there were staff that also had not had much to do with rabbits and took a whole lot away from the experience.

Kate and the staff also arranged a special day, where the Fire Brigade rolled into the school. Chris was made up. We have some amazing photos of him, dressed up in full uniform and sat in the driver's seat. As he was already quite a tall boy, he did not look out of place at all. He could easily have been mistaken for the driver that steered the tender into the school grounds. It didn't finish there as the hoses were connected up and those that were physically able could have a go at aiming the water at certain targets. I wasn't there on the day but have been reassured many times how much our son enjoyed the experience.

Other days, actually called career days included a policeman bringing in his motorcycle and the pupils were able to take it in turns to sit on the bike and set the Blues and Twos going.

Yet another time when Chris spent time with Martyn was very special. Martyn had the patience to strip down the wheel of a car and show Chris how to change the brake pads. There are not many people out there that would go the extra mile with a child that has severe autism. Martyn, you were very special to Chris, and you will always have our full respect. I trust that you are still working just as hard today as you were then. I'll have the pleasure, in another chapter to bring to you the way that this same man, came up with something new every sports day and kept us all entertained.

I once suggested to Kate that it would be rather nice for the kids if they had their own chickens to look after, to get to learn where eggs come from, to help collect them. Once again Kate listened and agreed to give it a go. The chickens remained at the school for a couple of years I think but I guess something happened, perhaps staff found it difficult to look after them, I'm not sure, but they were moved on. Probably my funniest memory about the chickens was when I was told about Christopher going in the kitchen and asking for tomatoes, which, if he was successful with his request, he would take them and throw them over the wire fence for the chickens. Whenever Chris did this it sent him into hysterical laughter.

As each Christmas approached, we looked forward to the school activities that would generate so much hard work for the staff and pupils alike. To get ready for a Carol service at the local church each class rehearsed tirelessly their own carols. It was tradition, as Christopher loved this time of year, to always buy him a new Christmas jumper in time for the Carol Service. The life of the jumper would be very dependent on his moods and behaviours and some years we had to buy a second jumper that he could wear on Christmas day. We could not deny our son this pleasure, he loved Christmas and for sure loved his Festive jumpers. On the day of the Carol service, all of the pupils that were physically able walked to the church, probably somewhere between one and two miles and after the service legged it back again. It was indeed a real pleasure to have received an invite each year. The quality of the service was amazing and put together in such a way that the children, despite their autism, appeared to know what it was all about. The singing and the playing of some musical instruments was so moving and a credit to the staff that had worked so hard with the production.

After the service all parents and dignitaries, including the vicar, were invited back to the school hall to mingle with the pupils and enjoy a mince pie and a glass or two of my favourite, non-alcoholic mulled wine. It was always such a pleasure because we got to meet with the two school chefs, such lovely people, a lady and gentleman that made no secret that they had a special affinity for Chris, they loved his cheeky smile as he often requested seconds. As far as I was concerned their coup de gras was their wonderful, mulled wine. You know they kept their recipe secret for more than two years, when they probably got fed up with me pestering them and told me how they made this very warming mixture. What made it so special was that no matter how many glasses you drank you knew you could drive home safely and not get nicked for drink driving. Incidentally the food they served every day to staff and residents was also first class. Thank you, Chefs.

Something else that needs a special mention about Christmas is what my dear wife did every year, no matter what school Christopher was attending.

Tina always made us such a beautiful Christmas cake and made an identical one that we took into Christopher. The themes were always different but were based on something that our son could easily relate to the festive period. Incidentally, not only did they look so wonderful, but they also had the most adoring flavour, helped by the extra few spoons of brandy that I sneaked into the mix when my wife's back was turned. Tina spends many hours making these cakes every year and gets great pleasure from it. Tina also makes Christopher's birthday cake every year. In fact she makes a beautiful birthday cake for each of the family. A very talented lady, with an artistic brilliance. Thank you, Tina, for making Christmas so special for Chris, the staff that look after him and of course us at home that have great pleasure in devouring your version of Mary Berry's Christmas cake recipe. It is one of my biggest reasons why I love Christmas every year.

Just about a five-minute drive from Hill House was the village shop and staff started to take Christopher there from time to time. The two middle aged ladies that owned the shop became very fond of our son and suggested that he might like to work in the shop for one afternoon each week, helping to serve and sweep up, anything in fact that Chris was able to do that would give him a purpose. It was decided that it was certainly worth trying and so each Thursday afternoon Chris would be driven to the shop and a carer would stay with him whilst he did his work. Even the customers loved our son. A lady came in one day and spotted Chris just staring at a bar of chocolate, not taking his eyes off it for a moment. What is amazing is that although he so wanted that chocolate bar, not once did he attempt to help himself, credit to him and staff at the school, they had taught him well. The lady that had been watching Chris decided she would like to buy a bar of chocolate and having paid our little man, she proceeded to give the chocolate bar back to him and told him to enjoy.

Always very polite, Chris remembered to say thank you, then devoured the sweet pretty quickly. Christopher continued to work at the shop for some while and I am never sure why he stopped. Perhaps he had done enough at the store and wanted something new. We actually had the pleasure of meeting the owners, two lovely caring ladies at the annual carol service. You know, I think they were heartbroken that Chris no longer worked for them every Thursday.

Hill House was always very special to us as you have probably gathered by now, but none more than on the day that a specialist psychiatrist, who the head teacher and the local psychiatrist had been talking to, travelled from up North to spend some time with our son. Can you honestly see that happening anywhere else. She had travelled over two hundred miles taking several hours.

As well as observing Chris, she spoke with us as well and at the end of the consultation came up with ideas that helped Christopher immensely. I'd say that's a very special lady that deserves some special recognition. Thank you.

Let me finish this chapter by telling you about one more person that brought the best out of Christopher. We made friends with the lady who was from Ireland and who was helping Chris with his Speech and language. She was always full of fun, and I could not resist one day when I gave her the nick name "Spud", based on her country of origin and that her surname, I think, was Murphy. She took no offence and showed she could take a joke or two. She taught Chris how to use a programme properly called Sonoflex that had been purchased for his I Pad. It was so useful and very similar to Pecs, but all done at the touch of buttons. It Meant that Chris could easily request things when he became tongue tied. I would really recommend it. Our son became almost expert on that programme. It helped keep him calm at times where he might have lost it. Thank you Spud for what you did for our son and for many others at the school.

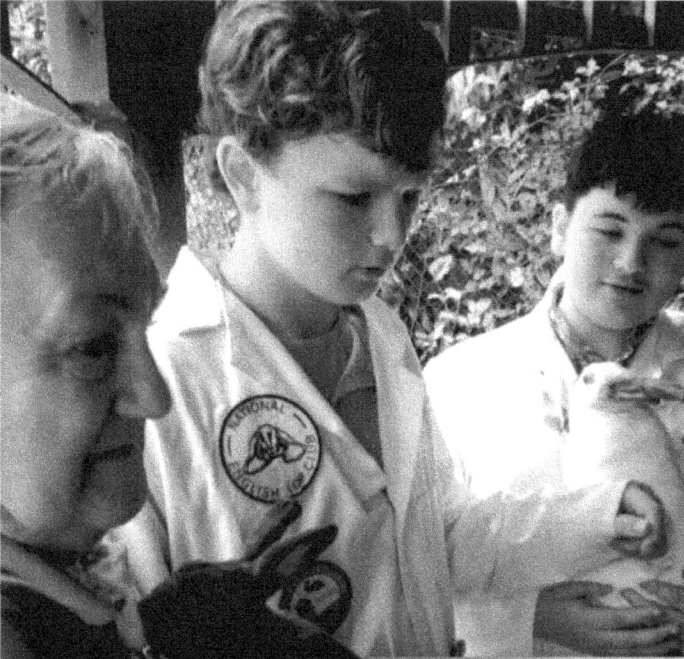

Left: *when we took some of our rabbits to Hill House School - with his brother Charlie and Dad.*

Right: *Aged 15 at Hill House Careers Day.*

At home enjoying a cup of tea with Mum and Dad.

Charles Parker

CHAPTER 13

Sports Days at Hill House

Every year, when getting towards the end of the summer term, Hill House would hold their Sports Day. Taking responsibility for each of these and the Star Performer was Martyn.

Every year the theme was something different but whatever it maybe there was only one man that starred, as I said Martyn, and he went to great lengths to see the whole thing was a success. The games he came up with were designed so that everyone one of the pupils, some with a little help, could take part.

Staff, including Kate the head teacher, would put their heads in the stocks so that everyone could have a go at getting them soaked, with wet sponges. I have to admire our older son Charlie, as he too put his neck on the line, or head in the stocks and seemed to appear to enjoy it when his brother, Chris and many others took turns at the throwing.

Another event that was never missed at sports day was the Tug of War. I don't think it mattered which side you chose to pull for but once the teams were sorted it was a deadly serious competition. It was in fact just great fun. There was hardly a dry eye, everyone seeing the funny side.

Now to remember some of the themes. There was Star Wars, Harry Potter and another year Wimbledon when crafty old Martyn got me involved. Martin was the star dressed as John McEnroe and we had one hell of a Singles Final. I most certainly was the most static tennis player seen in any final, having had a knee operation many years back that was nothing but trouble. I don't remember who won, that did not matter. Once again, Martyn did a brilliant job and stole the number one spot on the day.

After the very first sports day that we attended at Hill House everything changed for the rest and for the better. Hill House, or Cambian the owners, invested heavily in the playground. It became something really special. A track, new swings and there were all sorts of new equipment that made it probably one of the finest facilities at a special needs school anywhere in the country. Christopher did not want to be anywhere else.

Some of those sports' days fell on extremely hot days in July but the school made sure there was an abundance of cold drinks available for everyone. I think it was five sports days that we attended, certainly four, although for the life of me I cannot remember the theme for one of them. It must have been so enjoyable that it blew me away, I'm sorry I just cannot recall.

As the actual sports came to an end, it really was only the beginning. Those two wonderful chefs at the school had been working hard all day preparing and cooking the most amazing barbeque food for everyone. Followed by strawberries and cream.

The barbeque was certainly Christopher's favourite part of the occasion but never underestimate the head teacher. Still to follow was an ice-cream for everyone, pupils, staff and guests. Kate arranged every year, for an ice-cream van to come to the school and serve each and all with an ice cream or lolly of their choice. What more could one ask for. What more could any parent want to see than their child enjoying themselves to the full. Once again thank you Kate, thank you Martyn and thank you to each and every staff member that played their part on those very special sports days.

Just recently someone shared something very special with me and I do hope it is true. I was told in fact that Hill House School in the New Forest is the only True Green school in the country. Congratulations to them for that achievement.

CHAPTER 14

The Family Fund

There is one thing for sure, when you have one or more children that are disabled it will undoubtedly mean you are going to do much more washing for example. Certainly, in the early days you will have an incontinence problem, greater than a normal child. In our case we have had a double whammy as our older son Charlie had a slow transiting bowel problem.

The point I am trying to make is that we were wearing out washing machines and dryers fairly quickly. There were various bits of furniture that were being broken up that needed replacing. Clothes and bedclothes that were being constantly torn to pieces by Christopher and soiled beyond repair. We constantly had our hand in our pocket buying and replacing all sorts.

I see that lately the Family Fund have been appearing on television, being sponsored which is absolutely wonderful. When we first learned about the Family Fund, they didn't have that help from sponsors, just funding from the government and yet somehow, they managed to help us so many times. Generally, one was allowed to make an application for their help once a year. It was a case of telling them what you needed and why and not being dishonest as there were always plenty more in need as well as our own family.

Each year we would make our application, generally requesting a little more than perhaps you needed but not being greedy. We found them to be so generous. Over the years we said thank you for their help for things like a new washing machine, a dryer, when the one we had caught fire, grants for clothes that Chris had ripped to pieces and bedclothes that were no longer usable. They supplied a trampoline one year for the boys and paid towards a holiday for the family, when things were getting very tight.

This may sound confusing, but we hated asking for help and sometimes would not do so, knowing how helpful the family fund had already been towards us. They put our minds to rest when they told us that the charity was running thanks to subsidies they received from the government.

With that explanation we didn't feel quite so bad. They also told us that so much specialist equipment that we would need and specially built and strengthened furniture would cost at least double or treble the price of the more common household chairs, tables and beds that may be required.

We were told, the Family fund is there for a purpose. Please do not be ashamed to use their help. Without the help of the Family Fund, I truly believe we would have struggled at times and without them I am absolutely certain that thousands of families would struggle, especially at these very difficult times when prices for everything are rocketing. My advice, if you are a bit like we were, almost embarrassed to ask for help is that you must swallow your pride right away, accept some help and just think that by accepting help how much better you are caring for your children.

So that you don't have to spend your time, wondering how you can contact this amazing organisation here is the link you can use, should you need it.

https://www.familyfund.org.uk

From the bottom of my heart to the Family Fund, I say a massive thank you, we have appreciated all of your help.

CHAPTER 15

Let's Eat

Let's Eat! It sounds like there's food involved and that always excites me.

This will not be a very long chapter but one that will always fill Tina and me with pride.

Kate, the head teacher at Hill House, always wanting to do something different and to keep up with the Jones's as the saying goes decided that what Hill House needed was a small café where pupils could go to and order what they would like for their lunch. It would give pupils what many never had. Choice. It empowered the pupils to have whatever they chose from the picture menu placed around on the walls. The pupils would have to remember to collect knives and forks when they got their food and to ask for any sauces that they wanted.

They had the space available, the funding to do the work but something was missing. A NAME for the student's café.

It was decided that this should be decided by those that were going to use the facility. Each pupil had the chance to write their choice of name on a ballot paper, place it into the secret ballot for everyone to vote on the favourite suggestion. What a great idea? A closing date was set and everyone was getting super excited about the name of their new "Hang Out".

We as parents were told nothing about this until after the result of the ballot and until the name had been engraved and safely fixed above the door.

On arrival at the school Kate asked us to go with her, she had something to show us. Oops, what had our son done, I thought?

We went through a couple of security gates and having done so, Kate revealed all about this wonder idea of hers, the new café. She of course then told us how the name had been decided and when asking us to look up, revealed it had been our son's suggestion that had won the day. How very special. How very simple and straightforward. Christopher's suggestion, his chosen name was "LETS EAT".

It wasn't long before we had the chance to grab some lunch ourselves from the café and it just felt so extra special to think that this place, so special to so many had been named by our son. "Let's Eat!" It said everything it had to in two very simple words. Christopher's Legacy. Proud of you Chrissy Boy.

What's even more wonderful is that the popularity of the café grew very quickly, so much so that the daily numbers outgrew the facility. Not to be beaten, Kate, the head teacher, knowing there was room for expansion, had builders on site without delay.

There is now plenty of space for all of the residents and the staff if they wish to fill their tummies at "Let's Eat".

CHAPTER 16

The Mystery Traveller

Early on the 20th October 2015, the three of us set off from our home destined for a holiday of a lifetime. We were going Down Under.

For many years the love of my life, Tina and I of course had worked so hard to deal with all of the behaviours we had thrown at us by a mixture of autism and anxiety. Christopher had needed extra special care from three years old, when he was diagnosed with severe autism and challenging behaviour. A little later ADHD was added to our son's problems. Very recently it has been confirmed that Chris also has Sensory processing disorder. Tina had suspected this to be the case for a while. Having it confirmed has made lots of what he does so much easier to understand.

Charlie, too, had some problems, a slow transiting bowel for one but in the main it was his acute anxiety and the attacks he had to endure from Christopher that meant he too needed lots of additional help. We had quite a shock recently when we found out from our doctor that Charlie had been diagnosed in 2008 with Aspergers Syndrome and us only finding that out in January 2023. It had been added to his notes, but no one had the courtesy to write to us and confirm. How on earth could this be? We know he had a diagnosis in 2008 but we had been told verbally that the result was negative. We shall probably never get to the truth and must rest on what our doctor has told us.

Tina and I had not had a break or holiday since 2003 when were able to take Charlie to Florida where we were able to spend some very special time with him, to be his mum and dad and to let him know he had every minute of every day devoted to him. You see whilst at home that was not the case when Christopher happened to be off school or home at the weekends. Charlie was almost too scared to come out of his bedroom for fear he would be attacked by his little brother. That holiday in Florida was truly wonderful and we saw Charlie really enjoy himself for the first time in many a day. He would be out in our very own pool that came with the ten-berth bungalow before we had even eaten our breakfast on most mornings. Being a wild animal fanatic and with our bungalow backing onto a wild game reserve Charlie was in his element. Look dad, look mum, he would shout, there's an armadillo or sometimes he would refer to an animal I had never heard of before. He certainly knew his stuff, that's for sure.

So, twelve years had passed since the Florida experience and Charlie had reached eighteen and said he wanted to do his own thing at home, with a carer or friend living in with him, if we decided to take a holiday. Even when we suggested he join us in Australia, his animal knowledge kicked in and reminded us of all the killer snakes and spiders, he was having none of that.

To have even thought about what I had in mind would have been impossible without Hill House School. I mean, how could we go away for a month and leave our autistic son with someone or some school that we could not trust. Most of the staff at Hill House loved Christopher almost as much as we did. We knew we could trust them. I remember Kate, the head teacher giving us her blessing. You go and enjoy yourselves and we'll stay in touch and rest assured Christopher will be fine.

One problem we had was to explain to Christopher that we were going on holiday and would not be visiting him for the next four Wednesday evenings.

Christopher helped us out somewhat. We knew of course that he liked drawing and on one particular day he drew this rather strange picture, perhaps part human, part animal, I did not have a clue. Christopher knew right away who he had drawn and when asked he said "ANK".

"Christopher", Tina asked, "would you like mummy and daddy to take Ank on holiday with us". Very swiftly came the one-word reply, "Yes". So it was, that we were taking Ank with us to the other side of the world, and we had vowed that we would make sure that every couple of days Ank would be in touch.

We ran the idea of taking a third person with us by Kate and she thought it was amazing. What a novel way to get Chris interested and have him look forward to hearing from his parents and his special friend. Tina got working on a small model of Ank that we would also take with us just in case our son's version got lost in the crowds. We kept our word to Christopher taking every chance to use Skype, Zoom and even Face Time to chat with him. Every occasion we touched base, Chris would ask after his friend. "Ank".

From the time we left home to getting back we had travelled almost thirty thousand miles. We had visited five of the seven states in Australia, preserved so many wonderful life time memories and achieved yet one more of my dreams.

My idea was, if we are doing this, going all the way down under, were going to do it in style, certainly to the best our money could buy. I thought that if we were going to spend so much time on a plane we needed it to be in comfort. We would go the whole way, well almost, business class and first class were non-starters, but we did book Premium seats on the four long haul flights that we would make on the holiday. As luck would have it, we did not have to spend as much as was first thought. The agent Aust Travel, had worked a miracle and got us premium seats for very little more than the cost of the more mundane, squashed together seats that were the alternative.

Having the extra room meant Ank could sit quite comfortably on Tina's lap and have plenty of pictures taken to prove he was enjoying the trip.

The flight, as you have probably gathered was split with a stop being made at Hong Kong both on the outward and the return trip. It meant that on arrival at Hong Kong we had about a two hour wait before taking off again on a different plane, destination Cairns some eleven hours away.

None of us, Tina, Ank or I had completed a flight quite this long before, but I have to say Cathay Pacific were amazing, we were shown very special care and excellent food and drink.

As we approached Cairns, the sun was still to rise but everything had been arranged by our agent in England and a taxi was waiting at the airport to take us on to our first hotel. Our first task was to get used to the heat. That first day, the beginning of a very special month in our lives took some getting used to. We were more than pleasantly surprised how friendly our host, the female manager of the hotel was and how she kindly took a stroll with us down to the sea. She showed us the best places to eat, the parts of the beach that we best avoid, because there were saltwater crocs in the sea where the water was deep enough. She didn't need to tell us twice.

Having spent a few days in Cairns it was off to the airport and our next flight would take us to Uluru or as most would know it Ayers Rock. The land of desert, the land of flies. I have never seen so many flies ever before. The first thing we bought was a fly net for each of our heads, mine bright blue and Tina's pink. What a Fly Net Selfie that made. We could not stop laughing when we spotted a group of foreign travellers, all wearing orange fly nets. We called them the Tango people, as if their purpose was to advertise the drink.

God, the temperature at Cairns was hot but at Ayers Rock it reached 42 degrees Centigrade. With climate change now a regular subject I do wonder if we shall ever experience temperatures like that here in the United Kingdom.

Something very funny happened on our trip to the rock. The light was falling and there was nothing but red sand all around us. I had two hearing aids, one blue and yes you have probably guessed the other was red. Guess which one I lost? Your right, the red one. What do I do now, nine thousand miles from home and with only half my hearing? Don't you believe it. Tina took Ank for a little walk, retraced our steps and after about fifteen, maybe twenty minutes she returned, with one red hearing aid. Now that is what I call a good set of eyes.

From Ayers Rock we flew south and spent a fantastic few days in Sydney, visiting the famous Bondi Beach where Tina added to her lovely bronze tan and I finished up with feet the colour of a lobster.

Thank goodness I didn't fall to sleep, I think I may have been cooked perhaps as much as medium rare or more.

It was then on another flight to Melbourne. The day after arrival was the biggest horse race in Melbourne, probably the biggest in the whole of Australia. It was also my birthday. As we sat having breakfast, we could see all of the ladies, spruced up in their refinery, looking fit to turn many a man's eye and obviously off to the races.

In Melbourne the weather was very much like ours in the UK and late in the afternoon it suddenly changed. The heavens opened up and it poured, much to the annoyance of all those ladies that had been racing and were now returning home or to their hotels. It may have annoyed the ladies but to us it was brilliant entertainment as we watched all of these bedraggled women scurrying along. None, or very few had the common sense to take an umbrella or a light raincoat. What made it even more amusing was the thought that many of the race punters, men and women, were probably out of pocket as the winner of the big race that day was a female jockey and probably not backed by too many.

Well having watched these drowned rats it was time to get on with my party. I think the agent back in the UK had let the hotel know that it was my birthday as drinks were on the house for the two of us, for most of the evening. We will never forget Melbourne.

Next was a flight to Adelaide where we again enjoyed a couple of days before taking a boat ride across to Kangaroo Island. Now wouldn't you think, the clue being in the name, that you would see lots of Roos on that Island.

Quite the opposite as apparently most of them found cool spots to hide away. We had a car on the island and drove virtually all around it in the two days we were there but had to wait till the afternoon we were due to get back on the boat before seeing a massive Boomer, a male Roo, standing in the middle of a field. What a sight, to actually see such a wonderful creature close up was just amazing. What was surprising to us was the number of large earth mounds along the side of the roads. We found out after that there are many Kangaroos in Australia that get hit by cars and lorries and rather than bury them, they just cover them with plenty of soil by the side of the road and they are there for eternity to remind drivers to be more careful.

Actually, you may not approve, but the closest we actually got to a kangaroo was on our plate one evening, we just had to try it. Delicious.

So it was back to Adelaide and after one more night there we flew to our last stop on that magnificent continent, Brisbane and the Great Barrier Reef. How amazing was that? It was hard to believe your eyes, but it was incredible. In fact the whole Australia experience had been just something else.

If I had to put my finger on three things that will forever stand out in my mind and remain in my memory it would be these. Our visit to an aboriginal village in the Blue Mountains, where we had our lunch cooked in Earth Ovens. Secondly to hold a Koala Bear, oh I wish I could have smuggled him back and the third and probably the coup de gras was when a mother roo allowed me the privilege of smoothing her Joey whilst in her pouch. There cannot be many that can recall having three such wonderful events happening in their life. Of course there were many more but far too many to tell you about right now.

Tina too, had her special moments and it would be unfair if I were not to share just few of them with you. The first was whilst at Steve Irwin's Zoo where she recalls seeing Big Al, a massive fourteen-foot Crocodile loose in the arena.

Tina's next memory was when on a water trip she saw a leather back turtle come to the surface, such a beautiful creature she told me and finally, her third stand out moment was having the privilege of sitting on the beach whilst all of the Little Penguins, that's their name and breed, made it on to shore and we were able to follow them back to their burrows. Like me, Tina remembers so many other fantastic things as well. We took hundreds of photographs and lots of video that we were able to share with our boys, our family and friends once we got home. Ank never actually shared his best moments with us but one thing for sure is that he cheered Christopher up every time he was spotted on zoom.

So, the last stretch of our fantastic venture, presents already bought and packed in our cases, we were soon to be on the first leg of the journey home. Like the outward flight we were again stopping off at Hong Kong but on the way home we had arranged to spend just a couple of days looking around the place that used to be a part of the United Kingdom. What a place Hong Kong proved to be, just a sensational place to spend the last forty-eight hours of our holiday, that was my special thank you to my beautiful wife for what she had done for both of our boys. Like me, I know Tina enjoyed it but both of us were ready to get home and see the boys and those that we had missed over the last month.

Unlike England where you may have a tailors shop next to a bakers and then maybe a travel agent, Hong Kong was different. There was a whole street where there was nothing but lights and lighting equipment on sale. Another street would have shops where poultry, chickens and ducks, hung by their necks, filled the windows. One thing that stood out in these shops was the number of bowls filled to the brim with chicken's feet, apparently a delicacy over there. The street we were looking for was the one where we could eat. A decent restaurant that we could trust and after seeking advice we went for a place that was renowned for its quality. We had a superb meal there and will never forget it. The memories of Australia and of Hong Kong are still as clear as day. Given the opportunity, but only if somehow, we could take Charlie and Christopher with us, we would go back down under tomorrow.

Oh, by the way, Ank informed us and told Chris on the many calls we had with him that he thoroughly enjoyed the trip.

Thank you for allowing me to share what was a very important part of our lives together. We were able to recharge our batteries, to spend premium time together that sometimes becomes very difficult under our circumstances when at home. Please remember this. Yes, we may have been away for a month, but we will never ever forget to put our boys and our family first.

CHAPTER 17

College at Hill House

Chris had been through all the years at Hill House and we were beginning to worry. What would be next!

We were absolutely delighted to hear that it wasn't time for our son too leave this amazing school just yet. He was going to complete at least one more year in the forest as he had been accepted at the Hill House College which gave us more time to find an adult placement.

Some days Chris would attend the college at Hill House whilst on others he would go to Brockenhurst College, just about a four-mile drive along the road. He had the chance to do all sorts of things between the two.

Brockenhurst gave him the opportunity to learn how to do brick laying. Never did I think I would see my son attempt this, let alone make such a good job of it. Even when another student started to become rather noisy, Christopher remained calm with his mind fully concentrated on the job in hand.

Back at Hill House Chris helped to make many useful garden ornaments out of wood. Bird tables were very popular, and our son became very confident at marking off timber cutting to size, with safe supervision and putting the screws in place to hold everything together. Once assembled every piece had to be painted with a preservative.

Planters, they were another useful garden item that was made at the college. They were obviously very popular as they could always been seen marked up for sale and at a very reasonable price. Certainly, value for money and all the profits going back into the school.

Probably the best thing for Christopher was that the Hill House College was in the main, on the same site as the school. He could make his own way there after he had breakfast, no need for transport. The only time he had any transport to college was on the days he attended Brockenhurst College.

One of the things that stood out at the Hill House College was the remarkable patience of the staff, tutors and carers as they had to do all of these jobs and carried them out brilliantly. Then, at something like the get together after the Christmas Carol Service, you had the opportunity to buy whatever had been made that term. You had to be extremely quick, nothing sat on the shelf, as the saying goes, for long. Talking for myself, it was the pride I had thinking I had bought something made by my son or others who attended college. That in itself made whatever it was very special. It immediately had a sentimental value to me and to many other parents or friends that were buying on the day.

One thing that was very special and I knew my younger grandchildren would love was a model of Olaf from the movie "Frozen". It was very cleverly made, looked realistic and was going nowhere other than my car boot, to find its way home and form a part of our festive decorations. Bidding on Olaf started slowly but then I got a little nervous as others came on board. I was taking no chances, as I answered the call for any more bids. Thirty Pounds, I said. The room went quiet all of a sudden, then erupted into loud clapping and cheering as the head teacher brought down the hammer and proclaimed "Sold, Thirty Pounds, Charles Parker.

I was elated, over the moon and that was more money in the school pot and I had something that Christopher and my grandchildren could enjoy that was quite unique. They in fact, loved Olaf. He actually made it through another couple of Christmas celebrations before he started looking really sorry for himself. It was bought for the kids and who was I deny them playing with him.

Christopher was taught so much at college and started to grow into a much calmer person, simply I believe, because he had received so much social interaction with his tutors and many of his fellow scholars. He could often be seen doing little jobs or errands around Hill House and appeared to be loving every moment. I truly believe and am so grateful to everyone at Hill House that with their hard work, their exceptional and intuitive caring they had given our son a real chance in life. He appeared to be able to manage many more of the problems that he had and although we knew as a family autism would never disappear, that our son had been given a fighting chance.

Of course, what would matter most was for us to find an adult placement that could carry on from where this wonderful school, buried in the heart of the New Forest, had brought Christopher over the last five years.

Having had so much confidence in Hill House we now were starting to worry once again. Would his next home, his first in adult care, be a one-year wonder or could it, as we hoped become his forever home.

Left: *Opening a present that "Ank" brought him from Australia.*

Right: *Chris with his Mum on our return from Australia.*

Cuddles with Dad and his Brother when we got back from Australia.

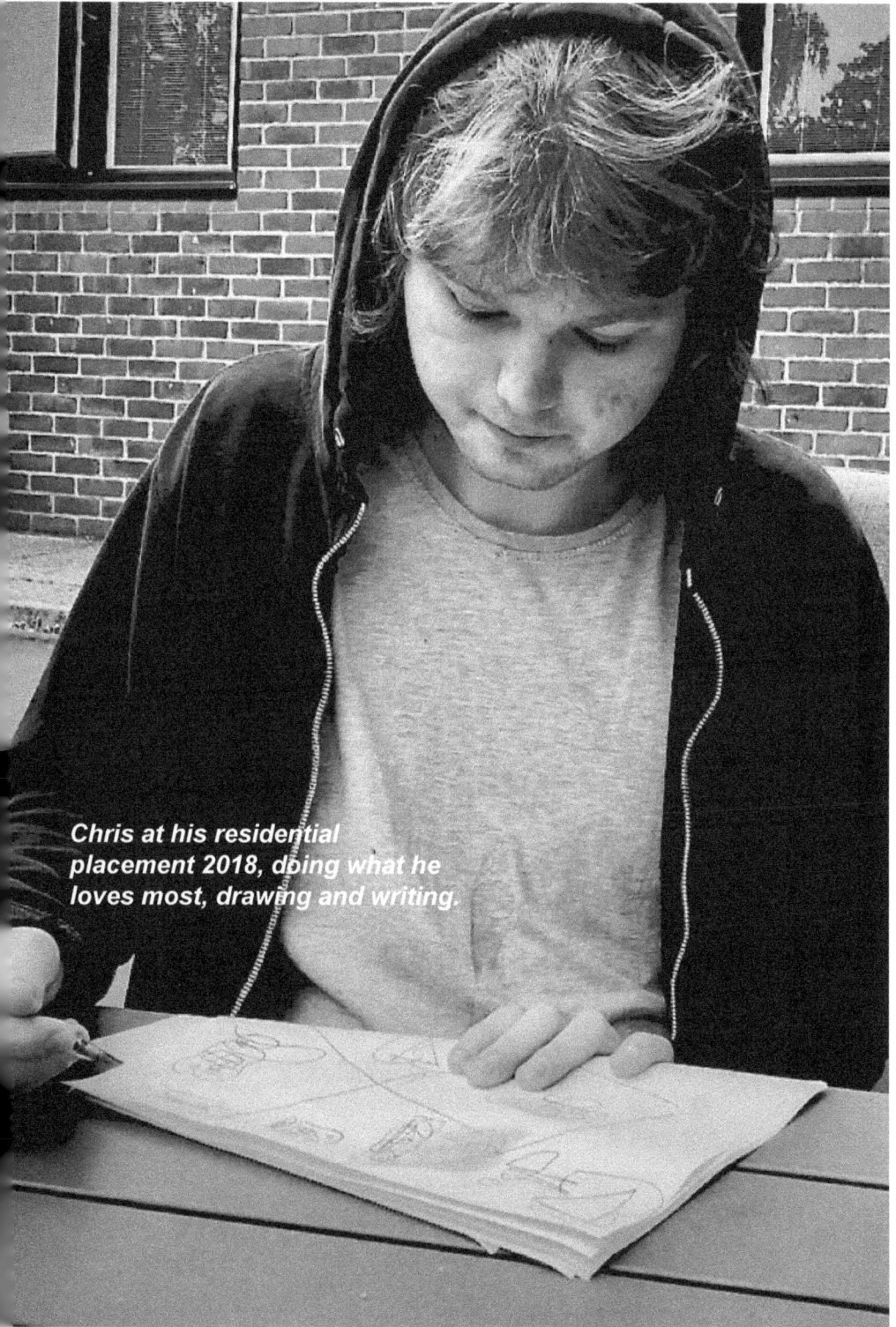

Chris at his residential placement 2018, doing what he loves most, drawing and writing.

CHAPTER 18

Would We Let Him Down Again

Having had the problems that arose at our son's three previous schools it does start to worry you and make you think. Whilst life for Christopher had been nothing short of amazing at Hill House, we now had to find somewhere, a residential placement, that would potentially become his forever home.   I suppose one could not help thinking about some of these questions.

Was it possible that some or all of the problems that Chris had at three out of his four of his schools would raise their ugly head again? Perhaps, but we would need to be alert and be able to recognise anything that might give us important clues.

Were the things that went wrong at these schools our fault? Perhaps, but I think more of the problem was a result of staff at these schools not listening to us and possibly not being given enough training. As parents and having started at the deep end, I believe we had so much valuable information to offer, that had staff listened it could have made so much difference to the outcome of so many issues. Another reason of course is that very often we found staff and carers that did not have enough experience. They could not understand a person like our son, with such serious and complicated problems.

Were we always too picky, bearing in mind that it was always our intention to find the best, probably not? As a parent you must obtain the best for your child. Failing to aim high, is surely without doubt, failing your loved one.

I will hold my hand up, as will my wife and admit that we did make some mistakes, elementary ones at that. Particularly when it came to choosing the Hilton over the Holiday Inn, you'll no doubt remember what I mean. Were we too impetuous, should we have asked more questions, thought about it all a lot more. At the end of the day, would it have changed our mind when we found out that Hill House had problems at that time resulting in a change of head teacher, just before Christopher was accepted there. As it happens, we may have done the right thing, for the years that Chris spent at Hill House were the best years of his life up to then. I think it is one we have to take on the chin, learn from it and pledge ourselves to Christopher and Charlie, promising that we will try to do better in the future.

I truly believe that every parent tries to do their best, sometimes being pushed into decisions, into schools that are the only ones available at the time. That was not the case with Tina and me, we were always ready to battle with the authorities and would not accept second best. Perhaps the proof of that was that we prepared for and fought three tribunals on behalf of our two boys.

Some people, including from the local authority, have asked, could you not have Christopher back home. The blunt answer to this is no but what it does tell us is that anyone who believes we could have Chris home has little or no comprehensive understanding of his problems. Neither do they give much thought to our other son Charlie, who because he was so often attacked by Chris, made us take the decision to turn to residential care. We were not going back there, that was for sure. It affected Charlie's mental health badly and he is still working hard to control the life it has left him with.

The time had almost arrived, just a few months before the inevitable. Christopher having to move on from the school he had learnt to love. The school that loved Chris and a school that had so far to him, changed his life and changed his educational attainments beyond all expectations.

When you think that on joining Hill House Chris was still on all of his "P" Levels and by the time he left he was clear of all of them. Yup, my boy, was to leave Hill House with levels for every subject on the National Curriculum. A massive thank you to all of his teachers, they were for sure, some extremely special people.

Without doubt, Hill House, compared to all of the schools he had attended was brilliant. We certainly had, saved the best for last.

But, and a very big BUT, when Christopher had to leave Hill House and move into adult care could we, his parents find a residential home that was equally as good as he had been used to for the last five years.

We had to start searching. Searching was something we had certainly been used to, but this was not a school we were hunting for, in reality it was our son's forever home.

In hindsight and due to only being given one option, a residential home, we made a massive mistake right at the outset of our search. Had we been informed that Supported Living was another option we would have seriously looked at that, for sure.

Supported living is where a property is either leased or purchased on behalf of the person, they live within the community wherever possible and have their own regular carers that they can learn to trust. That's it in the shell of a nut but I will go into this further as we venture on.

At this stage, as I said, residential was our only option. Where should we look? That was our first thought and certainly no easy answer came to mind.

Tina and I started by looking online, searching for residential establishments that looked good, were in the right geographical area and whose informational pamphlet attracted us the most. It was important, as I was reminded by Tina, that we must make no assumptions by just reading information, we needed to visit all homes that we felt might have a chance of offering our son what he needed. To ask as many questions as possible that were needed and not, certainly not to make any rash decisions. We would do our best to ensure no more mistakes or decisions were made just because somewhere looked nice.

We had eleven residential homes on our list and it was a case of calling each one, asking if they had any vacancies, if not immediately, then in a few months. If we got a positive answer to our first question the next was to ask when we could visit and take a look around.

It was to be a very difficult task for us. To help we had prepared a whole host of questions to which we would expect to get honest answers. One home that Chris would have certainly liked was just a few hundred yards from Bournemouth beach. The downside from the home's view was that all of the residents were young ladies and that worried them. Minds were made up when we happened to mention that our son could be rather loud. Staff were then worried that the noise may upset neighbours and their opinions were important.

Another of the homes we had to visit, was in fact, just about three miles from where we lived, it would have been ideal, but they could not be sure they would have a room available and were concerned a little about Christopher's challenging behaviours. It was indeed a shame, it was a lovely place, had a friendly feel to it and somewhere that we thought Chris would be happy. Within easy distance, it would have meant that we could visit regularly and could have brought our son home for lunch or dinner with the help of carers, whenever he wanted to visit us. Never mind, for the time being it was another we must cross off of our list.

Each of the homes we looked at were different and yet still had many similarities, does that make sense. Some were ideally situated, whilst others were almost in a town centre.

One that we visited, in a rural area, with a massive garden had previously been the home of one of Southampton's football players. Of course, they get bought by a bigger club and their off to pastures anew. It was really stately, massive rooms and apart from one thing, would have suited Christopher. All of the residents were nonverbal, and whilst this was not their fault, it may have proved detrimental to Christopher's progress. The very thing we would not want was any possible regression, especially after he was about to leave his final school where he had done so well. For the time being this home was put on the back burner.

Some of the other homes we looked at were not as described and would definitely not be suitable for our son. We could take no risks. It actually left us with two options. One at Ashurst on the edge of the New Forest and a new home, not even ready yet as it was in the middle of being renovated.

We decided to look at the one in Ashurst first, which had for a long time been under the same management, The Cambian Group, as Christopher's school, Hill House. That was until Cambian decided to sell off all of their adult homes and concentrate on the schools that they were doing so well with. It was a lovely home, within walking distance of the New Forest. Massive rooms and a very large garden but one thing bothered us a whole lot. We were worried that one of the residents was blind and we could not predict how our son might react to the lad. We talked lots about it, both between ourselves and the manager at the home. In the end our minds were made up for us as the young lady that was scheduled leave had changed her mind, meaning her room was no longer available.

Well, we started with eleven and now had one home left to view. Would it have what we were looking for? We had booked an appointment for the following week and just had to be patient.

Whilst waiting to look at this last home, we did our best to find out as much as possible on the internet. We found that the home was owned and run a very reputable company, with a high long-standing reputation.

On the day arranged we travelled to north Hampshire, a journey for us of around forty miles to fifty miles. When we arrived, we saw a reasonably new building that was still being worked on.

We were met by a friendly guy who explained that the home still needed quite a bit of work done to it before it was ready to take residents. However, we could see the potential. There were two flats on the ground floor, each of which had a beautiful kitchen and they had already been finished. As well as the kitchen each flat had a lounge, bathroom and bedroom. Right away we mentioned that one of the flats, rather than just a room upstairs is what we would prefer for Christopher. One flat had already been taken but the other was available. So, the gentleman, agreed that providing that when he and a colleague did the assessment on Christopher everything was fine and that funding could be agreed, in principle the flat could be our sons. We took a look around the garden, saw what was to be a sensory room and looked at the upstairs where there were four bedrooms and a communal kitchen.

We wanted that remaining flat for our son and before we left pushed the person into agreeing a date with Hill House when the assessment would take place. It was arranged for the following week. The assessors would visit Chris at Hill House in the morning and would then visit us in the afternoon. Arriving at our home around 3pm. They asked us numerous questions, making many notes in the process. We too asked for a whole lot more information then after about two hours the gentlemen left.

We then had to wait and find out if they could look after our son and if funding would be available. It wasn't too bad actually for within a couple of weeks we had the good news. Christopher had been accepted. In hindsight I wonder if the amount of funding our son could generate had anything to do with that decision. Here, there was an empty home, apart from one flat that was taken and I guess they needed money coming in as quickly as possible.

That, however, was not our problem, we had found what we thought at the time was an amazing home where our son would spend his future.

Perhaps one downside was the fact that it would mean us making about a one-hundred-mile round journey every time we visited Chris at his new home but rest assured that distance could have been double. If the placement was right for our son, then distance was not even on our minds.

It was then a case of waiting for the home to be completed and for the transition plan to be written up, before Chris could make this massive move into adult care.

CHAPTER 19

Be Your Childs Voice

If you have a child or children in your family that are on the autistic spectrum or if they have any mental illness or lack capacity that prevents them from making their own decisions this chapter is probably the most important and I beg you to read and digest it fully.

Late in 2016 we realised that once Christopher reached eighteen years old, he would be an adult. In very simple terms that meant that the day before his birthday we would still be his parents and could make decisions for him. On the day he became eighteen, as parents it meant that we had limited rights and that if we were not careful the local authority could step in and make decisions instead of us.

With what has happened since our son's coming of age, thank goodness we made the decision to apply to become Christopher's legal deputies, both for Property and Finance and for Health and Welfare.

We could just apply to become a Power of Attorney for our son, but it does not carry the weight of a deputyship. If you are unsure contact a solicitor, preferably one that specialises in the subject.

Can it be expensive to become a legal deputy? Yes, it can but let me ask you a question or two.

When your child becomes an adult do you still want to be responsible for them, to make decisions for them if they are unable?

Or do you want someone that barely knows your child, someone like a social worker to be making decisions for your child and perhaps interfering in your family lives.

Trust me, they will sometimes still try to take over when you have a deputyship, but you do then have the court on your side.

To obtain the position of Deputy does require lots of forms to be completed. I actually completed the forms for our application but if you don't have the confidence then either employ a solicitor or perhaps ask around amongst your friends. Maybe one of them has already made an application for someone in their family and would be able to help you. Of course, you could also contact me and I will help to complete the application.

Once you are granted your deputyship by a judge, you will be expected to submit an annual return to the Office of the Public Guardian each year. On the documents you are sent, it will tell you what you can and cannot do but if you're not sure seek advice, perhaps by calling the Office of the Public Guardian. They are very understanding and very helpful.

Believe me when I say that it is not that difficult, just a few forms and the OPG staff are always willing to offer advice. One piece of advice that I can offer is to keep good records of any money you receive or spend on your child's behalf. It's also a good idea, if your child does not have a bank account of their own, to get one and you will need to be the signatory. With these things in place it makes keeping records so much easier.

We have found the Office of the Public Guardian extremely helpful and quite recently they have pointed us in the right direction as to where to get the extra help we required.

Another thing to remember is that if your child is on low income as most are, you can apply on their behalf for a remission of fees or a complete exemption.

To be able to make decisions on your child's behalf is important. To stop others making those decisions instead of you is paramount to the future of the person you are representing and that you love.

Of course, if you are reading my book in another country there may be different systems in place, but I am sure very similar legal rules, systems and ideas will apply. In this case I would suggest you talk to a good solicitor that will be able to help.

Something else you will need to do on behalf of the person you are caring for is to look after their benefits. Most, by the time they are eighteen, will no doubt be getting either DLA, Disability Living Allowance or PIPS. If they are not, then do not waste any more time. Get the forms and apply. You have nothing to lose.

Something else and equally as important is to claim Universal Credit. For this you will need to visit the local job centre but will not in the first instant have to take the claimant, especially if you hold a deputyship document for Property and Finance. It is also possible as we found out for Christopher to increase the Universal Credit payment. If you can prove that your "Charge" has no immediate hope of working, then you can make application for the Limited Capacity to Work benefit. This part of the benefit is only paid to those that meet the criteria but can make a real difference to their income. Do remember also that DLA and PIPS are not liable to tax and will therefore not make any difference to the taxable income of your son or daughter.

For those that have problems such as Aspergers and are looking for support and help, perhaps with applying for employment or help attending employment, a really good organisation to contact is the National Autistic Society.

I do hope that this chapter, although fairly short, has been of interest but more importantly useful to you.

CHAPTER 20

The Next Big Step - His Forever Home

This next step was massive, and Tina and I, although really excited could not stop thinking, had we got it right?

There was a date set for Chris to start his transition and move into his forever home but then came a setback. Whilst almost all of the work was complete, the placement had yet to get the all clear from the CQC, that's Care Quality Commission, in other words to be signed off and approved. That meant a delay and we were not sure how long Chris would have to wait, which meant he would stay at Hill House a little longer. In honesty I do not think Christopher cared and certainly the staff that had grown so close to our son were more than happy to keep him for a while longer.

We were visiting Hill House one day and we were shocked. By the time of this visit everyone knew when Chris would make the move. All of the staff and us included were asked not to mention anything about the date in front of our lad.

He didn't need telling, he already knew, and he told us. Christopher moving on twentieth of August, he said. So, how did he find out. It transpires that someone had left a letter on a desk about Chris and his move. Obviously thinking it was safe, for one thing it was not facing up the right way for anyone to read. Except our son, Christopher. He could read well and on that particular day the staff found out that our young man could also read anything upside-down.

Dealing with the transition then had to be carefully planned and social stories would be all important.

On one of the transition visits, we met the Hill House staff and Chris at the home. We had arranged for us all to eat lunch together and we had brought with us fish and chips that would be cooked from frozen in the main kitchen by the staff. Looking back, I do think, with what they were going to be paid every month that the lunch should have been on them. Never mind.

There was only time for Chris to visit his new home once more before the August date and he did this with just the Hill House staff.

We had booked a long way up front, to take Charlie to Edinburgh Zoo and to go to the Edinburgh Tattoo and our time away would coincide with Chris moving. As it happened, that was fine because we had been asked not visit Chris for at least two weeks. Brilliant, although we would worry and probably think of nothing else with Christopher in the back of our minds, it did mean we could once again spend some precious time with Charlie.

We were still in Edinburgh when we received a phone call from the manager at the new home. "Sorry I have to bother you", she said. "You know the brand-new television you bought for Chris and the special protective frame you had made for it, well I am afraid he has pulled it off the wall and smashed it up".

Shocked, not really the right word but let's stick with that. How on earth was he allowed to do that, where were his carers. The television and the bespoke frame came to close on one thousand pounds and now it was no more. The only explanation we got is that he made a "b" line for it, was quicker than his carers and that was that. It is difficult to understand that even if he pulled it off the wall, why didn't his carers move in to stop the total obliteration. In hindsight maybe we should have waited a while before introducing the television; we just wanted our son, who was new to that home and knew no one, to have something special.

Incidentally, waiting for the two weeks before visiting Chris went out of the window. Before even leaving Edinburgh, we were asked to visit as soon as we could upon our return home, Chris was clearly missing us, perhaps wondering if he would ever see us again. It would take us three days to get back home as we had a stopover booked for one night, about halfway, at the same Air B and B we had used on the way up to Scotland, just to break the long journey.

Such was the importance of visiting our son we decided that once we arrived home from Scotland, we would freshen up and be on our way. Christopher was so relieved to see us, he cried and to be honest and I felt that way too. Already I was questioning whether we had made the right choice, although having looked at ten other homes, we were not left with a lot of choice.

There was, what I would call a very shallow explanation about the television and frame, and it made us very wary about introducing anything else at that time. Were these carers up to the mark?

In fact, something that we found out more than four years after Chris had moved in, was that one of carers only started there the same day as our son and that he had never worked in the Care Industry before. How disgusting was that.

How did we find out that information? Well, it was from that same person, the newbie carer but he did not tell us until after he had left the home. One thing he did to make progress was to talk to us lots about Chris. He also worked hard, trained hard and as it happened turned out to be a fantastic carer. What's more is that he hit it off with Chris and they had a wonderful understanding of each other. We were so sad when he told us that he was leaving but we understood completely when we learnt of the trials and tribulations he was put through by the management at that home.

Incidentally, I am delighted to tell you that same person is now doing really well; he is now a manager in a reputable care company that offers supported living. Well done, young man, you deserve a massive thank you for what you achieved with our son.

We continued at the residential home as we had left off at Hill House School by visiting Chris every Wednesday afternoon and taking him for his customary drive out and visit to MacDonalds, which he absolutely. loved.

One thing particularly worried us and worried us even more when we were constantly being asked to provide new clothes for Christopher. He appeared to be tearing up, not just his clothes but also bed clothes, faster than we could replace them. As you can imagine, this was very expensive, some months costing as much as one hundred and fifty pounds. Weighted blankets, that Chris loved, could cost up to eighty pounds. Why did this tearing and destruction suddenly get so bad? Every behaviour tells a story, what was Chris trying to tell us?

Yes, Chris did tear his clothes at Hill House from time to time but not on the same scale. We had to discover why and what was causing the acceleration with his tearing? Obviously autistic people do not like change. Could it be his way of demonstrating about his recent move? Could it be more than that? Did he not like it at this new home?

We were really careful to take in everything we saw and heard from his carers and somethings bothered us. On one particular day we were shocked. Chris was very upset and was crying. Foolishly his carer said something to him that has stuck with him ever since that day. "Don't cry Christopher, Crying is bad." My wife, Tina, immediately jumped on this, first by telling Christopher that it was alright to cry, everyone cries son and then she turned to the carer and told him never to repeat that statement. We reported the matter to the manager but even that fell on deaf ears. It was obvious that staff had not been told of the damage in that one statement that one of their colleagues had caused. How do we know that, because since that day we have heard others say exactly same thing to Christopher.

What we did notice is that Christopher was not being encouraged to use his PECS book, that had travelled with him from Hill House. This was our son's way of communicating when he could not give any clues verbally. When we asked staff at the home, they knew nothing about the whereabouts of the PECS book and that did little to give us any belief they were even looking for it.

It was not until after Covid and we were allowed back into Christopher's flat, some three years later, that the mystery was solved, and it was obvious that no one had looked very hard. We found the missing communications book in one of Christopher's kitchen cupboards, still with the note inside the front cover that Hill House had placed there almost three years previous. Another explanation found, without even one word having been spoken.

On the same day we found that all important book, we decided to have a sniff around to see what else we could turn up. On the top of the kitchen units we could see what looked like wrapping paper. Standing on a chair my wife discovered unopened Christmas presents that we had left on Christmas day two years previous, so that our son had some bits and pieces to open later on Christmas day, when we had left to go home. We meant later that Christmas day of course, not two years later. We immediately let Chris open them all, around ten different presents. Of course, the management knew nothing about why the presents had been hidden away. Not only had staff at the home kept his presents from him, but they had also taken away his voice by just putting his PECS book in a cupboard and basically forgetting about it.

This made us delve even further into what Hill House School had sent through to the home to ensure that Christopher's transition and ongoing life ran smoothly. At Hill House our son used a NOW and NEXT system. Written on his blackboard by Chris, was what he wanted to do now and what he wanted to do next. It worked brilliantly. Once those two were complete he would write the next two on his board. That way he always knew what he was doing. Any more than two would be too much.

All of this system was written within a document called an Environmental Report, produced by the Occupational Therapist, OT for short, and travelled with Christopher to the home with the remainder of his paperwork. Now, one of two things happened with this report. Perhaps the management had a quick look and filed it away or they just did not spend any time studying the report and implementing the contents. There is not much difference between our two assumptions, but one thing is for sure, our son certainly suffered. It was obvious because none of the suggestions, including Now and Next had been used with Christopher.

It was not until a long time after when Thornbury Nurses started to care for Chris that they regularly encouraged him to use the Now and Next System. Guess what? When Thornbury nurses were removed from Karibu some eighteen months later by the ICB and Local Authority because of funding and staff from the home were reinstated, the Now and Next system virtually disappeared again over night.

This will tell a story. When we picked up on this and spoke with the OT and Speech and Language therapists attached to the County Council, they asked the management at the home to get the Now and Next system up and running as quickly as possible. Instead of asking Chris to write his now and next on the board, they wrote twenty-four tasks on the blackboard and asked our son to choose from that list. It was obvious they did not have a clue what they were doing. The Occupational Therapist I have just mentioned would either call the home herself every month or ask her apprentice to do so, to ask if our son needed any help or intervention. The answer received was always the same. No, he's fine thank you. Yet it was so obvious that Christopher was desperate for that help. You will be pleased to read that as soon as we made contact with the OT and found out what happened and made her aware that Chris did need her help that she made an appointment right away and has been in regular contact with our son ever since.

It was, thank the Lord, a blessing that during the Covid Lock Down, that we had been using a communication tool called Zoom for quite a while with our online business. We could not physically visit Chris for months and we knew that would be very difficult for him, so we would arrange zoom meetings as often as possible with Christopher. At least that way he could see and hear us and it would help with his anxiety. Sometimes the Zoom would only last a minute or two, dependent on Chrissy's mood but I am sure it helped him. It certainly helped Tina and me, as we were missing Chris so badly. It was so worrying not seeing our son, not being able to hug him and perhaps more importantly not being able to keep an ear to the ground and know what was going on. We were and still are so proud of how Christopher coped with Covid. Tina did a lovely picture social story, explaining the bug as best she could, and we sent it to him.

Eventually, with lockdown lifted to a degree, we were able to visit Christopher but only outside. We had to dress up like plastic mummies but didn't mind that just as long as we could spend some time with our son. We had to take Covid tests every time before visiting and on arrival at the home have our temperature checked. Obviously, we were not permitted to take him for his drive but did the next best thing by picking up a MacDonald's meal on the way and sitting with him in the garden whilst he ate it.

Incidentally, the garden was a mess. There was a small canvas canopy in one corner but because of the state of it we could not use it. To call it filthy would have been flattering.

Somewhere between 2020 and 2021, the home was taken over by a new management company and we thought that perhaps things would improve. Neither improvements nor any decline was obvious right away but after a while we were thinking, how wrong can you be? Had we made yet another mistake? With the takeover various staff changes were made and unfortunately those changes started a faster demise of the care at the home, than we had hoped. Perhaps the most significant change was that the registered manager at the home was promoted to area manager, when someone left, to move on to a completely new company and therefore left the position free. That meant a new Registered manager had to be found, together with a deputy. It soon became obvious that neither of those appointed were cut out for the jobs and yet they are still there to this day. When you read on and find out what they were responsible for in relation to our son, you too, will be disgusted.

The changes were not, I'm afraid in the best interest of the residents at the home, at least not in my opinion. It was not long before two really good carers had left for pastures anew and we had indications that more and more agency staff were being used. Consistency, when looking after people with autism is so important. So too is experience. I remember, looking back to the school in Dorset when we had an admission from one carer on their first day in the job, that only the previous day they had been working at Burger King. You just do not know what you will get with agency staff, what training they have had, what experience they have, if any.

One of the carers that decided to leave was heartbroken, he loved Christopher and looked after him as if he were his own. The feelings were mutual, Chris really got on well with his key worker and was very upset when we had to tell him that his regular carer would be no more. I refer of course to the same gentleman I mentioned earlier, who had started at that home the same day as

Chris. We heard a whisper that the registered manager did not like the fact that this particular carer got on so well with us. You see we found out that from the very first day that person started work at the home, he was put to work with Christopher. As I also told you it was his first day ever working as a carer and he was not given much training at all.

Therefore, that gentleman and he deserves that title, he was in my mind a true gentleman, wanted to know how best to work with Chris, so he asked those that knew best, his mother and father. What was wrong with that. That same guy, that gentleman, since leaving the home and joining another has done so well. So well that I learnt only recently that he has earned a significant promotion with his new employers. Well Done Matey. I know I have repeated myself, but I believe I have the licence to do so, particularly with something so important that proves that staff were employed without any significant training. Is that what my son and others at that home deserved?

After his key worker had left, we started to feel that Christopher was not being looked after, quite as well as he should. There were no signs that the Now and next system had even been implemented let alone helping our son.

At around the same time as the staff changes, May 2021, we noticed that Christopher's self-injurious injuries were starting to rise. He was picking at his skin and hitting himself. When we arrived for our regular visit on a Wednesday afternoon, we could barely recognise our son. His face was swollen and very badly bruised. The swelling and the bruising were such that at first, I found it difficult to see that it was my son. Was this honestly something he could have inflicted on himself? We asked to see a report, but none was forthcoming. It would seem that no matter what accidents happened at the home the chances of receiving an incident report were very rare. We took photographs of Christopher on that day and every time I see them, I feel like crying. Our poor little lad looked so sad. Even as I write about this, I feel several emotions. Sadness because our son deserved better, guilt because I partly felt responsible for placing our son there and I tried so hard to feel the pain that he must have been going through. I have cried myself to sleep on many a night, when pictures of Christopher, looking like a beat-up boxer, flash up before me.

If Chris ever has any thought that his mum and dad were responsible, then I ask for his forgiveness. With this and things you will read about in a future chapter I do hope, you the reader of this true story will realise just how hard we have fought for our son, not just for a short time but for the whole of his life, ever since he was diagnosed with autism. I just think life can be so unfair and I know there are many people in this world worse off than our son but personally I see anyone in his situation, with severe autism, challenging behaviour and ADHD as serving a life sentence. Perhaps you do not agree, it is just my personal opinion, formed when I think what my son might have achieved in his life had he not had these problems. A very strong, fit young man whom we believe his intelligence to be masked by the autism.

Something very significant had happened not long after Christopher had moved into this home. We found out that he was not allowed to use the beautiful kitchen he had in his flat. All of his food was being cooked in the main kitchen upstairs and Christopher was being escorted to that area to eat all of his meals. Why was this?

If we are truthful, there were two main reasons why we wanted to get Chris fixed up with one of the two flats.at this home. Firstly, that it would give him the opportunity to live like any other young adult, learning to be independent within their own four walls, providing he got good care and support.

Secondly, the reason for so wanting one of the flats for Chris was the amazing kitchen. What an opportunity that fantastic kitchen would give him. He loved cooking, had been supported at Hill House to do plenty of cooking and we wanted that to continue.

Why were we not told the kitchen, or more specifically the cooker was a no-go area before we agreed to Chris moving in? I fully believe they had no intention of allowing the kitchens to be used in each of the flats, for fear they would be messed up and devalue the property. I believe, when the two guys who conducted the assessment spent so much time talking about how Chris would be able to do as much cooking as he liked they probably knew the truth. If not, I apologise. When we first viewed the home, only one flat was taken. The company must have been desperate to fill the other places to start getting money coming in. I also believe that when they realised how much Christopher could be worth to them, they saw the pound signs flash up before their eyes. Maybe I am wrong, and of course it is a business they are running not a charity.

We shall probably never know the truth.

CHAPTER 21

Dogs Bite Chris

What I am hoping to do in this chapter is to lighten things up a little. To tell you more about the funny side of our son. Many people I think, don't think, well that's what I think!

They perhaps, do not think that a person with autism can see the funny side, that they have no sense of humour. If our Chris is anything to go by, then I can assure you that there must be thousands, perhaps millions of autistic people out there across our planet that would prove that theory wrong.

Much of what I write about in this chapter will have some connection with animals. Some funny, some perhaps that have scared Christopher.

Other things that are certainly funny in hindsight but not at the time. Know from experience that when Christopher says to you, "WHAT HAVE YOU DONE", you need to on the alert. It will almost certainly be something he will laugh at but not something to which you would approve.

Let's first of all take a look at dogs. From a very young lad, Chris has been frightened by dogs. Tina and I worked so very hard to get Chris used to dogs, to learn that they could be friendly and were very unlikely to hurt anyone. When Chris was five, six maybe even seven we used to take him out to a park near to the beach in our city. He would sit quite happily in the buggy until he saw a dog. You may be wondering, couldn't Chris walk? Yes, he could but the buggy was his sanctity. He felt safe in it. On odd occasions when we thought we would risk going into town, it was a case of take him in the buggy or not at all. Without the buggy he could get worked up over nothing, flop to the floor and you had to carry him back to the car screaming. At least with the buggy, he might scream but at least you could quickly and safely get back to the car.

So, if we were out with our lad in the buggy and he saw a dog all hell would let lose until we came up with the idea of having a blanket ready to cover over him. Get passed the dog, remove the blanket, problem solved.

As Chris grew, I took him out some Saturdays with a Carer, we were gradually getting him used to dogs, I'd say we were winning. Until a woman came along with her dog off the lead, even though there were signs everywhere saying, dogs must be kept on the lead. Quite politely I asked if she would mind putting her dog back on the lead. I explained why but was immediately met with a barrage of rude words. During my conversation with the ignorant lady her dog kept running towards Christopher and all he could do was scream. That ignorant selfish person ruined everything we had worked so hard for and still to this day our son is scared of dogs. Hence the saying, Dogs will bite Chris. Thank you, Madam.

We are still pursuing some different ways of winning Chris over with dogs It may take many more years, but we will not give up.

Earlier in the book I spoke about a carer called Nelli, the most amazing person in the care industry that I have had the good fortune to meet and learn from her. Just a few weeks ago we were out walking with Chris and low and behold along came two dogs with their owners. What I witnessed was truly amazing. Nelli, first in a very calm voice reassured Chris, then gave him a great big hug as the dogs got closer. She continued to hug Chris and talk to him until we were all safely past the dogs. Christopher's reaction was to stay calm. I tell you, the Queen, although it's not her fault, very often gave the gongs to the wrong people or for the wrong reasons. I'm sure all the nominees deserve their recognition, but there are so many ordinary and yet special people that unfortunately get overlooked.

Just a few weeks ago a new thing for Christopher. He scared me out of my skin. We were taking Chris out for a drive, Tina, Nelli and me, then suddenly Chris made the loudest Moooooooo sound you could imagine. Apparently when Nelli had been taking Chris out she had been getting him to make different animal noises. They came across a herd of dairy cows, which Nelli directed Chris to look at as she asked him what noise they make. Ever since then, when he is driven past the same field or any other field that has cows in it, not only does Chris moo but he makes everyone else in the vehicle make the same noise. I tell you, the first time it made me jump out of my skin; now I just find it so funny.

Whenever Chris says something like "Cats will bite Chris", we turn it round to a positive, so our answer to that would be "Cats eat Cat food". Now he knows the answers so now we only give half the answer. Cats eat…… and he will complete the sentence with cat food. So, you can imagine if he talks about dogs biting, we just say, Dogs will eat…….and he says dog food. The real fun comes when Chris says, "Lions will bite Chris" and our reply, "No Chris, Lions eat… and he is quick to tell us the answer, Lion Bars.

Having watched so many movies in his day, Chris quite often comes out with sayings that he has heard every time he watches that movie again. Some of those include, "Watch your Fingers", "Why you crafty buggers". We might nonchalantly say, "Eggs from Heaven" and Christopher's immediate reply is "No from their bum". Another is "Chickens are revolting" so, so funny and he knows so many of these amusing sayings. Just give him a quote and he will tell you what movie it was from.

Something else that Chris often does is to sing some of the lyrics from a song, usually one he has again heard on a movie. Probably his favourite from Madagascar that he will sing, or more accurately shout goes something like the following. "I like to move it, move it. Then Chris would expect us to sing it back. He would have the last word, however. Waiting for us to finish, he would shout as loudly as possible, "Move It". This interaction does so much good, it is always so heart-warming and funny at the same time. Unfortunately, with Nelli no longer supporting Chris entertainment like this is not encouraged unless it comes from his dear old mum and dad.

When Christopher was somewhat younger, he started to recognise different colours, including that people indeed had different skin colours. So innocently he would point to a person and say, "It is Orange", or "it is Pink". With a black person however it took him a while to get that right, he would say "It is Brown". The very first time he said this was to a black carer who had come to take him out one weekend. I have to admire that guy, he took no offence whatsoever, replying, "That's right Chris, I am brown", not even trying to change the colour to black. Bless you Fungi, Chris still talks about you today.

Saying NO! Christopher's way of telling us no for many years was through his behaviour, usually a bad behaviour. Then he learnt the word no and more importantly what it meant. He was in fact about fifteen years old when he got his head around "NO" and now uses it quite often saying the word in a very loud and well pronounced manner. We are now able to fully understand Chris when he does not want to do something, to go somewhere or even to refuse to eat and drink what we have offered. It is so easy for us to take for granted such a simple word, no, one that actually does have such a massive meaning. Two little letters, N and O.

I must tell you Christopher recently came up with a new room freshener. It truly was so funny and yet so effective if you like onions. In his kitchen he found an onion, goodness knows what it was doing there, he would never use one to my knowledge. Picking the onion up he brought it through to his lounge threw it on the floor and straight away jumped on it, squashing it into little pieces. It actually refreshed the air in the lounge quite nicely. Perhaps he has come up with a new and relatively easy way to make your rooms smell nice.

Back to some of our pets now, our cats who Chris knows quite well. Ask him their names and although it is a long time in between seeing them Chris will tell you that they are Tommy and Timmy and that they are brothers.

We used to breed and show rabbits and from time to time took them to Hill House so that all of the residents could smooth them and feed them snacks. It took time for some of them to pluck up courage but most times the majority of the children wanted to be a part of the experience. Now Chris, you had to watch him when at home, he would open up hutches, letting the bunnies out and sometimes we would spot him walking off up the garden carrying a rabbit by its ears. Not the right way I know but trust me none of them came to any harm.

Now tell me, how many of you have had to tie a rope around your freezer. Our little man, for a while was rather naughty when you were off guard. He knew exactly when to make his move. Then he would say, "What have you done", or "the poo goes in the freezer" and that is exactly what he had done. After throwing away a fair amount of food for health reasons we put a stop to his antics by tying the lid of the freezer tight using some strong rope. What else could we do? You know, you really wanted to get cross but his cheeky smile and the thought that if you make big of it would only encourage him more. The rope did a good job, except when our other son Charlie, wanted a lolly or ice-cream and he could not untie the rope. His answer was to find some scissors and gradually work his way through the rope until he had access. You may think, why didn't we stop him? Just like Chris, Charlie knew how to time his attack on the rope. He knew that lots of our time would be spent on keeping a close eye on his brother and with the freezer in a small spare room, it was not somewhere that we visited too often. Charlie had his refreshment, we had to find more rope. Did I blame Charlie, not at all? If I am honest, I secretly, in my mind, congratulated him for his ingenuity.

Other somewhat dangerous things, that meant we had to have an isolator switch fitted high up in the kitchen included Chris putting biro pens in the toaster, CDs in the microwave, in fact anything that he thought would make him satisfied and allow him to say to us his familiar phrase, "What have you done". He was more than happy if he had wound up his mum and dad. The big problem for us was not making it obvious that we were a little bit annoyed and keeping a straight face when you knew full well smiling or laughing at what he had done would only promote more of the same. That was more difficult than you might think when you have a young man with a smile as broad as a Cheshire cat. Another thing that Chris has developed and is equally as amusing is his great big belly laugh, that comes out in as deep a voice as he can manage.

I do hope you have enjoyed this chapter. I hope it has brought a smile or two to your face. That's important if you are going to continue reading this book to the end because there are plenty more stories that will remove that smile as quickly as it appeared. However, who can say now that people with Autism have no sense of humour?

CHAPTER 22

Our World Comes Tumbling Down

Things at the home that we once thought was the cat's whiskers, were not perfect, we had experienced many different moments when we knew that Christopher was not getting treated properly and that in all probability our son was not happy.

His favourite carer, the only Person on site that appeared to know how to best help Chris, had got disillusioned with the management and left. Chris most likely felt abandoned. Many of his carers were new to him, most straight in from the agency but as parents and indeed Deputies you hope that everything will get better. Did they, you ask? I fear not. It was towards the latter part of October 2021, when it came to light that something very bad, very serious had occurred but not over just one day. The Cardinal Sin had happened over a period of twenty-two days. Now if this same mistake had happened at a hospital on just one or maybe two days, someone's head would have rolled. At the very least someone would have been suspended and placed under investigation, yet it appears to this day nothing has been done, except maybe a reprimand.

At this point I want to tell you that it is the registered manager's responsibility to see that all medication is given correctly, the right dosage and that it is given to the correct resident.

So what happened during those days in late October 2021 with our son's medication. Get ready to be shocked. For twenty-two days, that's forty-four doses, our son was not given his prescribed anti-psychotic medication.

HOW DISGUSTING IS THAT?

In short terms Christopher was forced to go cold Turkey. Having studied the effects, let me tell you some more. Firstly, if you come off too quickly you are much more like to have a relapse of your psychotic symptoms and may also increase the risk of developing tardive psychosis. Not that I am a doctor, but I have read that withdrawal symptoms can also include vomiting, nausea, diarrhoea, difficulty in sleeping, restlessness, anxiety, agitation and muscle movement including involuntary muscle contractions to name but a few. Interestingly you will see anxiety and restlessness on my list. Since this happened to Christopher, his psychiatrist has had to prescribe medication for prolonged anxiety and depression.

Now let me share with you some of the symptoms you may endure when anti-psychotic drugs are reintroduced to a person, which Chris had to get used to after missing those forty-four doses. I have read that a person starting or being reintroduced to anti-psychotic drugs may experience drowsiness, agitation, dry mouth, blurred vision, emotional blunting, dizziness and stuffy nose. I ask one question and have asked it many times since this happened to my son.

How is the person responsible for this disgusting misdemeanour still working at the home?

There are many other questions I would like to raise but at present we have a solicitor preparing papers for a case against the home and therefore it would not be wise to interfere with the work of our legal representative.

As if missing Christopher's medication was not enough, I have news, yes, there is more.

Again, I will not enter into too many details but on the 31st October our son had an accident at the home, damaging his arm very badly, skin and flesh being torn away. My wife and I did not receive an email to tell us of the injury until Tuesday 2nd November and what was worse, it was not until Wednesday 3rd November 2021 that the registered manager called for medical help. What's worse is that a paramedic only attended that day, when my wife and I happened to be there at the home for a meeting, saw the injury and insisted a doctor be called.

When a paramedic attended, he told us the injury was very dangerous and that it was very probable that sepsis had already started to set in. A prescription for antibiotics was written immediately and thank God the injury was caught just in time. The same question as before comes to mind.

How is the person responsible still working at the home?

As I mentioned we were at the home for a meeting about Christopher and at the same meeting was the NHS Commissioner for Hampshire who was also our son's case manager and when she heard of the two matters, I have told you about already and just one more that I want to share with you, she immediately placed the home under investigation and Safeguarding measures were introduced.

A question was immediately cast over the manager and about the ability of the staff at the home to keep our son safe. We were also very grateful that the commissioner also contacted Thornbury Nursing, authorising them to take over our son's care and confirming that carers from the home that had been looking after Chris should no longer have any contact with him. Thornbury nurses are very specialised and worked hard with Chris to correct the regression that was beginning to be obvious to most. We had been helped before by Thornbury when Chris was just fifteen years old and he was expelled from the school in Dorset just two days before the six-week summer break. We had learnt enough to know that if anyone was going to help our son it was indeed the carers from Thornbury.

So, the third issue, something else that we uncovered during that meeting. I asked the registered manager why we did not receive any accident report forms from the home, for we knew they happened. Just take the one I mentioned that occurred earlier in the year, in May, where our son inflicted severe injury to his face. An accident report form was never sent to us, so we must assume that such a form was never produced.

I was not happy with the response from the registered manager and asked that we be given, before we left the home that day, a full body map, conducted by two members of staff, not one. When we received the body map, you could have knocked me over with a feather. Get ready for this! The body map showed a total of thirteen, yes thirteen bruises on Christopher's body, none of which had been recorded, none of which had been reported to us, to the Commissioner or to the head of Safeguarding. It was also established that none of the bruises were positioned such, where they could have been self-inflicted. You must have guessed by now what I asked myself next?

How is the person responsible still working at the home?

There are many other matters that our solicitor is seeking explanations for, up to twelve at the last count.

What mattered from that day on was the urgent decision made to move our son to a new home, where he could be properly cared for and where he could feel safe. That we knew would not be easy, but it had to happen and quickly.

Within days of the meeting in early November, the Commissioner had kept her word, Grade 5 mental health nurses from Thornbury Nursing had started working with our son. Interestingly enough, and as I mentioned a short while back, we knew how good Thornbury nurses were and so had every confidence in them.

To be honest, it was like chalk and cheese between what Christopher had been used to up to the last week or so to what Thornbury were now providing. We very quickly saw an improvement in our son's behaviours, especially when the Thornbury office started to send regular nurses and Chris grew used to them. The commissioner assured us that Thornbury staff would continue to support Christopher until he had been found a new home.

Of course, with the matter reported to Safeguarding it followed that the CQC, that's Care Quality Control would visit together with the police for an inspection. Without going into too much detail the inspection took place and what we expected to happen, to what was the final outcome, turned out to be miles apart.

At first the CQC were going to downgrade the home on three matters but in the end settled on reprimanding the home for just Safety. I cannot for the life of me work out how they came to their decision. They in fact promised they would look at it all again, but I don't think that has or will ever happen. I suppose what I do hope is that when my book reaches you and hopefully many more that as members of the public you will make your voice heard and ask whether our CQC, put in place to protect, needs a dam good overall.

Until Christopher's court case is settled, and I am led to believe that it may be a while yet, I have to be very careful. One day though, and I am sure the day will come when we have proved our point, won our case, I and many others will be able to speak more freely.

Having made our minds up that his current home was definitely not good enough for Christopher, that the management and staff could not be trusted and that our son's future was definitely not there it was time to start searching again.

This would not be easy. The NHS Commissioner was on the case following up on homes that we had found and given her their details. A number of residential homes indicated that may be able to accommodate our son but then decided otherwise. It would have been very helpful if they had not kept us waiting so long. One, that we had great hopes for, had said that they thought that Chris would fit in but then kept us waiting on a shoestring as it were for over eight weeks before telling us that we would have to look elsewhere. Visits and interviews were made to homes from as far afield as the New Forest to

Bordon in North Hampshire but after high hopes, nothing conclusive came from any of them.

During our searches for residential accommodation something both sad and inconvenient happened. We were informed that the NHS Commissioner had contracted Covid and for the time being her place would be taken by another lady. That meant within the course of six to eight weeks, both our Social Worker and NHS Commissioner had been replaced. We understand why the social worker had moved on, it was for personal reasons to be closer to her young son during the day.

It is yet another story with the NHS Commissioner. When I asked after the health of the lady that had already helped my wife and I so much, or I asked when she would be returning, I was met with a blank screen, so to speak. All I was asked to do was not send her any more emails. You know, I absolutely dislike people that cannot be straight with you. Had the person that had done so much to help our son been sacked, had she been moved to one side or even requested that she be removed from Christopher's case.

Whatever the answer, I fully believe having worked so hard with that person and that both my wife and I trusted her and felt almost like friends the very least her senior could do was tell us the truth.

Her replacement leaves a lot to be desired to be as good. Unfortunately, she upsets me because her and her boss appear to think that I am below them, that they can simply say what they think is right and that my wife and I, on behalf of Christopher, will fall into line.

What I do not think either of these ladies, both working for the CCG, now changed to the ICB, do not understand, is that my worst hate is social snobbery. I will always respect anyone's position in life but will not respect the person that treats me as someone lower than they are. Social snobbery should be pushed down a deep hole and buried. As I see it, we all come into this world equal and we shall all leave it as equals. No one has the right to assume that by having an authoritarian attitude they force their views upon you. I will admit at some meetings, I do lose it a little. There are two reasons for that, the first being my passion about doing the best for my son and the second because I feel that some people in positions where they think they are better than you and they want their way or nothing, deserve to know that I for one will not be pushed around.

As deputies for my son, Tina and I work very hard. In fact, having submitted our annual returns a few weeks ago to the Office of The Public Guardian we were so pleasantly surprised to be commended about doing such a good job when they sent us their reply. They offered some great advice, assured us of their help, should we need it and have arranged an urgent meeting where we can discuss our concerns about some of these so-called officials that put themselves above us.

It is just my opinion, but I do think that if people in positions within a local authority were to treat others with the same respect as they expect themselves many problems, issues, call them what you wish, would be resolved much more quickly.

As for finding Christopher his for ever home, we shall continue searching but having tried looking at or asking over seventy-five residential homes without any joy whatsoever we believe we have to aim our efforts in another direction. Something that is now being encouraged by government and is fast becoming very popular.

Unfortunately, it does still need the help and co-operation of the local authority and the NHS, if like Christopher most of your funding comes from them. It is Supported Living, where a suitable property is found, and support workers employed to do the caring. One can either rent a property or purchase one with the help from some special agencies. I will tell you about both as I continue to write but for now must spend much of my time hunting for the right answer.

Incidentally, I have a secret to unfold about why that wonderful lady, so intent on seeing our son was cared for properly, was no longer in the job. She had been seriously ill with Covid and Long Covid but was then ordered by her senior to get rid of Thornbury nurses, they were costing far too much. When they were sent packing, carers at the home, the ones responsible for the neglect and abuse, mainly agency staff were to be reintroduced to Chris. Such was the passion of the commissioner for Chris and rather than do as she was told and cause our son more problems, she resigned her position.

Word reached us about the changes that would set Chris back and we, without delay, having taken advice, employed two very experienced London Solicitors. I will go into more detail about this in a later chapter.

You will read, as I continue with my story how difficult the local authority and NHS have become, even though we have presented them with an opportunity to save a colossal amount of taxpayer's money, whilst ensuring a home that would be safe for our young man.

CHAPTER 23

Choices

If I may, I would like to put you on the spot for a moment. Let me ask you a few questions. How important is Choice to you? How often, during the course of a day, do you change your mind? Maybe you change your mind about what you want for breakfast, lunch, dinner and even supper. You might change your mind about a drink, about what clothes you will wear, whether you might have a shower, a bath or just a quick wash with the flannel in the hand basin.

Let's carry on thinking about what choices we might make. Will you listen to the radio, if so, which radio station will you choose today or will it be the television this evening and if so again you have a choice of probably at least one hundred channels. Maybe you don't want either the radio or the television and that you choose to listen to some relaxing music, maybe head banging loud music, the choices again are massive.

Just a few more choices if you don't mind. If you live on your own, will you invite a friend round for the evening? Would you prefer to visit someone at their home? If on the other hand you are married with children, are you prepared to accept what your partner might like to eat, drink, or do in their spare time.

By now I think you will have understood that as "Normal People" our choices or decisions we have to make each and every day run into hundreds, may be thousands. In reality our choices are endless.

Now let's look at how you might be affected if you had all of your choices taken away. Would it make your life hard if you were not allowed any choices? Would it make you angry if someone else made every decision in your life for you? Would it make you sad, depressed or perhaps make you think about expressing your feelings through a behaviour?

Our son has been in four schools and currently in a residential home as you have learnt by reading this far. Save for his time at Hill House school Christopher has had his choices restricted, perhaps rationed. Perhaps at times, removed altogether.   At his schools, staff probably did their best to offer Christopher choices, but they would never have been quite as free as we find, choosing whatever we want and whenever we want something.

At his current residential home choices have for sure been very restricted. Some of that of course is caused by Dols, that stands for Deprivation of Liberty and means that any person in a secure school, residential home or secure unit are held under certain rules, perhaps what could be classed as the most detrimental is that they cannot of their own free will leave their home or school on their own, so there's a major choice gone, but one must realise you could never allow anyone like Christopher to just wonder off without someone with him.

Let me now compare many of your choices or even my own with those that my son has to enjoy. I know my son has a choice of sorts what he has for breakfast but for his lunch and dinner there is little or no choice at all. At my son's home, up until recently residents did not even have a menu, except for a written list. Tell me, how can an autistic person, perhaps one that is nonverbal and cannot read be expected to make an easy choice. They need lovely pictures that tell all, then there is a chance that they can make a choice.

Surely, I often ask myself, if a home is collecting over four thousand pounds a week for each resident, is it not possible to invest in some decent menus and at least give a choice of two or three meals for each lunch and dinner. It really is nothing short of a disgrace. Let me give you just one example of a Sunday dinner, that my wife and I witnessed just a few weeks ago.

Our son, perhaps in the minority, maybe not, has at his own choice might I add, been used to a roast dinner on Sundays. Not just roast, it had to be roast chicken when he used to come home at weekends. That was his choice and he would check the fridge the moment he arrived home on a Friday afternoon to see that the chicken was in place ready.

On this particular Sunday at the residential home, we had been out for a drive with Chris and thank God he had insisted on having something from MacDonalds because when his roast dinner arrived, back at the home, it wasn't. What I mean is that it was not a roast dinner. It was a plate of dry pasta, no obvious sauce, with a few spoons of garden peas mixed in. This was then followed by a jelly.

There are six residents at the home and if they all had the same, you do not need to be a top mathematician to work out the total cost for all six meals was probably less than ten pounds, perhaps even half of that. Where was the choice for this meal? In fact, where was the nutrition and perhaps even more importantly where was the thought for those residents when deciding for them that this was dinner today.

Something that decides how complicated a Sunday dinner will be is decided by who is working on that particular day. You see, the home does not employ a chef on a Saturday or Sunday. It just happens to be who is deemed to be in charge.

Thank goodness that during the time Thornbury staff looked after our son they worked hard to offer him as many choices as they could. However, they could not control the meal choices for lunch and dinner. Some of the Thornbury carers bring their lunch in with them, often a curry and they make sure they have made enough to share with Chris as they know curry is one of his absolute favourites.

Another way of giving someone like Christopher choice is to have a Now and Next Board and a Choice Board. They choose what they want to do now and write it down and also write down what they want to do next. That way structure is added to their day. They just need to be encouraged to continue writing down their now and next and providing it is their choice each time you are helping them to be more independent.

It is a fact that you can enable or disable someone by doing too much for them. It might be easier to go ahead and make a cup of tea for Christopher but what has he learned. Talking Chris through each stage of making his tea is helping him and eventually he will be able to make his own cup of tea.

It is a little bit like an analogy I once heard. A father was worried about his son getting enough to eat and so spent several hours each day catching a fish that his son could cook and therefore not go hungry. Now, if the father had spent some of that time teaching his son how to fish, he would never have to worry about his son going hungry ever again.

Another good example of helping Chris would be with the washing up, teaching and showing him every stage; that is helping someone.

You know, I learnt a while back how to tell a good carer from someone who is not really up for the job. A good carer has the ability to teach a person how to do tasks, how to help, to move them forward. A carer that is not as good will always look to take the easy way out and do everything themselves. That means they have done nothing whatsoever to help the person that most needs it.

To be helping Christopher his carers should be always looking to add new and exciting choices to the choice board. Things that will teach Christopher new skills, that will empower him to recognise the need to want more choice in his life and to implement them.

It is important, I believe, to understand that a lack of choice leads to boredom and boredom usually leads to a behaviour. Almost certainly a bad behaviour.

Finally, just think, how interesting, how exciting, would our own lives be if someone came along and took away all of our choices. How would that affect our mental health? We must always be prepared to give our children, indeed all of our family, whether they have any inflictions or not, one thing in their lives. CHOICE.

CHAPTER 24

Managing Behaviours

Without any doubt whatsoever in my mind, managing the behaviours of our son or indeed any autistic child is fully reliant on the person that is caring at the time and the first and most important thing for any Carer is to have an understanding of the person and how behaviours can develop.

Before Thornbury were asked to take over the care for our son, there was very little understanding of Christopher's behaviours since he had left Hill House School. An important way to reduce bad behaviours and encourage quite the opposite is for a Carer to have meaningful interaction with Christopher. It all comes down to trust.

Why does Christopher get on so well with the Thornbury Nurses? He trusts them, well most of them, one cannot say for sure how he feels about each and every one of them. Thornbury staff, have the ability to read into what may happen, to deal with a problem before it happens. That is the sign of someone that knows their job inside out. They know how to recognise antecedents, the problems, or reasons for the behaviour.

Just like those teachers and carers at Hill House, who had built up a fantastic rapport with Chris. In turn our son trusted those same very special people, they kept him busy, he was enjoying his life and so there was little need for him to speak through a behaviour.

This understanding, demonstrated at Hill House was definitely not happening anywhere near enough at the residential home prior to the arrival of Thornbury. In fact, after being asked to complete day sheets by filling in details of what was done with our son for every hour of every day for a period of eighteen days it was found, as I believe I may have mentioned before, that only 2.62% was deemed to be meaningful interaction. Hence, boredom crept in more and more and from that, bad behaviours, including breaking windows with his head that occurred on more than one occasion.

It proved that the staff at that time were not experienced enough in the field of caring, that they had no idea of how to redirect Chris when he desperately needed it. Without help with Now and Next and some other useful protocols Christopher was easily confused, he had no idea what he was expected to do with his time. He could not come up with ideas himself, other than some that were certainly not acceptable.

When Thornbury Nurses took over, they quickly discovered why many of the behaviours were happening and started to work very closely with our son, so that he nearly always knew what was expected of him.

Now and next, operating on his blackboard made an enormous difference, tearing of his clothes gradually reduced and attacking staff became almost a thing of the past. I certainly think that one of the most important things that helped Thornbury was the daily communication that they began having with us, the parents. They made a point to ask us as much as possible during the five-to-ten-minute period we had agreed to allot to these calls. We started to see amazing improvements in our son. Why, might you ask? Well, he was now being looked after by professionals, Grade five mental health nurses, that often worked in hospitals and the difference in approach towards Christopher was unrecognisable from what we had seen at any time by other staff at the home.

As I told you, back a few chapters, Thornbury Nurses are expensive and with two working with Christopher all day and another covering the night shift, our Local Authority wanted to cut costs. They in fact wanted to remove all of the Thornbury nurses and put back staff from the home that had been responsible for so many terrible things. We could not let this happen. I spoke with a very knowledgeable lady that was already involved in offering us some help and advice. She agreed with Tina and I and got in touch with two extremely experienced and qualified London solicitors.

After listening to us, they agreed that the withdrawal of these expert nurses could have a catastrophic effect on the care and future of our son. They wrote to the management of the home and to our Local Authority and made it very clear that any attempt to remove Thornbury would result in a Judicial Review. We heard after a while that the Local Authority, the CCG, had agreed that the present arrangement should stay in place until a new home was found for Christopher.

The arrangement was fine for a few more weeks, then we were called to yet another meeting, the first face to face meeting with the CCG and management of the home since before Covid had started. At that meeting they told us that it was their intention to remove one of the Thornbury nurses working the day shift and, in their place, put one of the staff from the home back in to work with Chris.

I tell you, I was up in arms, this had all been worked out well before the meeting. We sought advice again from our solicitors and after the assurance that Thornbury Nurses would remain in charge, we agreed that the Thornbury staff on the day shift could be reduced, with one staff member from the home taking that place. The CCG or Local Authority said at the meeting that it would give staff at the home the opportunity to learn from Thornbury. What a cheek I thought. Tina and I agreed but have been very diligent in monitoring what has happened since.

When we challenged the authorities and told them straight that the staff employed by the care home were not competent enough or trained enough to work with Christopher, they said they would arrange training to take place. It was arranged that three professionals including a Senior Occupational Therapist and Christopher's Speech and language Therapist would conduct a morning's training. One morning! In reality two hours maximum. I ask you what the staff at the home could be expected to learn in that time.

Tina and I knew that this would probably be a complete waste of time and so decided to attend the training, in order that we could help answer any questions that might arise. The people doing the training were brilliant but not so those receiving the training. Eight staff members from the home turned up. Not one of them had a notebook and after a short while one fell asleep so in affect there were seven. The training lasted just over two hours and at the end of it I asked when the next session would take place.

I was told by the Occupational Therapist, a fantastic lady that spent hours with our son, that was it. Two hours training and it was assumed the staff knew it all. I also asked how the rest of the staff that were either caring at the time or on days off would learn from the training. A manager from the home who was one of the seven piped up, "Oh, well we know it all now, we can teach the rest of them" WHAT AN ABSOLUTE JOKE.

The local authority continues and quite regularly to say that all the staff at the home had now been trained and know what to do. How disgusting is that. They, that is the authority had taken the word of the registered manager that all staff were sufficiently trained. This is the same woman that had let our son down so badly. I truly believe and I am raising the point with the Ombudsman that to ensure all staff were trained properly a member of the ICB or a social worker should have been present at the training.

We noticed something that happened directly after the finish of that face-to-face meeting that told us so much. How much in fact, that was being decided by holding what the CCG thought were secret meetings. Unfortunately, we were on to them. We spotted the senior manager of the CCG and the senior manager of the local authority, make their way to two of the senior management of the company that owned Christopher's care home. They escorted these people to another room and so the secret meeting began. It was quite obvious to Tina and me that this not-so-secret meeting had been convened in order to make arrangements for the changes about to happen.

Do these people at the CCG and Local Authority think that we are idiots? You know, sometimes, judging by the way they try to make decisions behind our backs that they do think exactly that. How disappointing for them that we are not idiots, that we will not just accept what they want, we will also stand firm to get the best for our son. I trust that many readers of this book will have the confidence to be same as us. Never become a pushover.

It does help you to understand why other people, who we have to deal with within those departments so often exclude us from meetings and try to implement things that should never happen without our approval.

How about this for an example. Although we are legal deputies, the new Case manager saw fit to go behind our backs, without the courtesy of telling us even, and appoint an advocate for our son. Did she not realise that we are indeed his advocates? Or did she think we were not good enough at what we did? The long and the short of this is that we complained so many times that after several months the advocate, who never once spoke to us, was removed.

It did not take long for us to recognise that Christopher had been affected by the change in the staff structure. Our son is no fool; yes, he has autism, but also has the most amazing memory. Perhaps he could recall how some of the staff that worked with him before the arrival of the Thornbury Nurses had treated him.

Staff at the home were meant to help, to work with Thornbury, yet on one Sunday when we took Chris for a lovely drive and then walk, I personally witnessed the person working for the home, drop off the pace, roll a cigarette and smoke it, whilst supposedly being on duty and helping the Thornbury nurse to look after Christopher. I immediately dropped back as well, so I could keep an eye on what this guy was up to.

On that day, Nelli was the Thornbury Carer and she and my wife Tina were some six hundred yards away, across the other side of a lake, such was the time taken out when this fellow rolled his cigarette and smoked it. If something major had happened what good would our smoker friend have been?

As it happened, there was an incident with two dogs. Having waited back to keep an eye on the chap enjoying his cigarette, it was Tina that witnessed and told me later how Nelli had handled two Doggie situations. You probably remember I told you a few chapters back about Nelli's expertise.

Our smoking guy's misdemeanours whilst on duty did not end there, however. When we were driving back to the home, Tina turned around to chat with Chris and could clearly see the Carer sat in the seat behind her, was texting on his mobile phone. He saw Tina had spotted him and rather than apologise tried to hide his phone between his legs. I ask? Is this why good money is paid, for people like that man to work with our son. Incidentally, I found out shortly afterwards that he was from an agency and had only been working at the home for two months. Certainly not long enough to have the experience to work with someone as severe and complex as our son.

On arrival home that day, I immediately wrote to the CCG, then registered and reported the day's events to Safeguarding. To this day, there has been no enquiry or reply. All, it would seem, covered up. I also wrote to the registered manager at the home, the one responsible for all of the injuries and neglect that my son had endured and told her that I did not wish for the smoking Carer to ever work again with my son. Did she take any notice? I guess not for a few weeks back that same guy was scheduled to work with Christopher as we were about to leave to go home. I spoke with the person in charge, requested that the staff be changed around and made it clear that my wife and I would not leave until my request was dealt with.

Something that worries us so much is the demise of our son and the increase of his negative behaviours since the local authority insisted that a Thornbury staff member be replaced with a Carer from the home. It has for sure put more pressure on the one Thornbury Nurse that remains to take care of Chris, for the help they get from the other Carer attached to the home is minimal. Most of those sit in a corner and make notes on a Tablet, rather than be a part of the package. I think one of the reasons is again, the lack of experience, the lack of training. There are one or two of those Carers that have recently looked like they are trying but not really injecting anything positive into our son's care package.

A sign that Chris is now confused about those caring for him is demonstrated by his upward trend of inappropriate behaviours. Since Thornbury have been stretched by having Carers working with them that are constantly changing every three hours, Christopher, by tearing more and more of his clothes is saying, "I am not happy". In fact, he so often says out loud, "Home is finished". Boy, I wish it was! I feel as Parents and Deputies and along with the CCG and Local Authority we are all failing a young man that deserves so much better. I just keep feeling that it is time for the authorities as a whole to be willing to work with us. Not to have that attitude that what we say goes. It is so unnecessary but seniors within the system do not see this or their staff as a problem.

What would help? It would most certainly help if the lady that was previously our NHS Commissioner and who worked so tirelessly with us for our son, were to miraculously reappear. That would without doubt help us and our son. Both Tina and I had the greatest respect for that lady and trusted her explicitly. I too believe that lady's respect for us was reciprocal.

Perhaps the most important message I can endorse at this point is that to manage Christopher's behaviours, and that is us included, we must build a trust that works both ways. Never, ever, show Christopher you are scared of an action, that you suspect may be imminent. Show him a positive way that he can move forward. Remember you are on his side, and he needs to feel that. If he just gets the smallest hint that you are worried or scared of what he might do, then he will almost certainly oblige by carrying on with the behaviour. If you are not sure what the right answer maybe, then ask for help or advice. I know there are times when decisions must be made on the spot, we have all faced those and sometimes made a mistake but wherever you can, use the chance to learn from a situation.

As I have mentioned already, how good, how experienced Nelli is when working with Chris. She does not mess around when she notices changes in our son's behaviours. She does something that is positive. Just a few weeks ago, Christopher's behavioural levels suddenly dipped and had been that way for a few days. Nelli's answer, was knowing how much Chris loves walking, to be out in the open away from the home to take him out at the first possible chance to somewhere he could walk and walk for as long as he wanted. The following day was no different, she assured Chris he was going out again and he did, to walk and walk some more. Over those two days' both Nelli and Christopher achieved over twenty-six thousand steps. The result, a much calmer young man. A fantastic carer had worked her magic again, by using meaningful interaction with Chris, she had put a stop to something that could have escalated very quickly. Yet again I have to say that experience told, well done Nelli.

Something, you may have noticed throughout my true-life story is that the tense in my writing changes and will do more from here as we still await a positive conclusion. I may pop back to the past, write in the present and even, at times, dare to look forward. I do hope you understand.

I spoke earlier in this chapter about not being afraid to stand up against the authorities if you believe you are right or that they are selling your child short in the care being offered. We had got to a point, where the case manager was making too many decisions off her own back, lying and blaming us for matters regarding our son and a new care company we had started talking to in the hope that they could help us in the future were not getting the support they needed. Instead, the case manager deliberately made out she had not received emails and information she had asked the carers for. Unfortunately for her, we had written evidence that this lady was wrong and we submitted an official complaint.

We were not surprised when we received answers that tried to vindicate the case manager, make excuses and in places blame us. So never to be ones to give up we are now taking our case to the governmental Ombudsman. It may take a very long time to get a decision and it may not be what we want to hear. If that is the case, we will ask the media if they would like to share our problem, we will not let it just fade away.

Oh, you may like to know, that we now have a new case worker, the third in just under two years. This time it is a young man, who up to now has been very helpful. Let us hope that continues. His predecessor has apparently moved on.

CHAPTER 25

Time To Think Again

Let me bring you up to date with the time that has elapsed since we first realised the urgency of moving Christopher from his present Residential Home into somewhere that we feel will be so much better for him. The appalling neglect and abuse towards our son happened towards the end of October and the beginning of November 2021.

I wrote most of this chapter in September 2022, so you can see that already ten months have gone by. Ten months where our poor lad has had to continue living in a residential home that has very little to offer, save for the Thornbury Nurses that care for him the best way they possibly can.

Whilst the home underwent an inspection by the CQC before Christmas, 2021, little has happened at the home to offer any reassurance to residents or their families that they might witness some improvements.

Something that Christopher is very reliant on and that makes a real difference to his behaviours every day, is transport to take him for rides and enable him to jump out in the countryside and take long walks. To enjoy this privilege, he has to depend on drivers from the home taking him out in their car, that is the car owned by the home. There are five other residents at the home that are all very reliant on drivers to take them out as well.

Christopher has had his own car, since I transferred my BMW into his name, but he is still awaiting help to finance the running of it. It's a bit of a thirsty motor and difficult for Chris to fill up until he gets some financial assistance that he had been promised by the Local Authority. As parents, we subsidise the vehicle as much as possible and take Chris out at least twice a week in the BMW or in any case whenever we visit. However, twice a week is not enough, he needs to be going out at least once every day. Some Mondays, when he is due to go swimming, he is unable to do so, again because there is no driver available or because the car owned by the home is in the garage again for repair, something that seems to happen all too often these days.

Having been in contact with some seventy-five residential homes, with very little joy on the horizon, we listened with interest to some other ideas, one of which is called Supported Living. The idea being that you or whoever has legal responsibility for your child, seek out a home that can either be secured on a long-term lease or purchased. Once you have the home in place, it is time to decide on the Carers you would like to attend to your son or daughter. Our preference to a long-term lease, or renting as many of you would recognise, is to purchase Christopher his own home using a special system that the government is encouraging. It is a little complex and I think it best if I tell you more about that in a separate chapter.

Let me direct you to some of the many advantages Christopher will enjoy once he has his own forever home with Carers that we choose to look after him.

Perhaps the first should be to tell you that Supported Living is perhaps the closest to the way that you and I live in our home. The one big difference being that our son, being severely autistic, will have regular Carers, appointed by us, being his Parents and Legal Deputies, to look after him every hour of every day. These will be fully trained Carers of course and it is our aim not to have any Agency staff involved save in extreme emergency. The Carers will also have to follow a daily routine that we agree with them, making sure that Christopher continues his Now and Next procedure that is currently used.

This ensures that our son has something very important and something that we are all entitled to, CHOICES, as I mentioned earlier. Just because a child or young adult has a health problem it does not mean that anyone has the right to take away their choice of what they wish to do next, where they want to go or what they want to eat.

Let me just make it clear, that some young adults may not need as much care as our son, maybe someone popping in two or three times each day, to help perhaps with chores they find more difficult.

So, the choice of Carers is vitally important as is the regularity that each Carer spends with Chris. We certainly do not want constant chopping and changing, which would do our son no favours at all. A small team of well trained, competent, and confident Carers is the answer and to achieve that you need to make your ideas clear to the management of the care company you have chosen. Do remember, it is what you want and what you know your child needs that counts.

As Legal Deputies we are able to make many decisions for our son but must still be compliant with any rules and conditions as laid down by the Court of Protection.

Tina and I have actually applied to the Local Authority to have a Personal Health Budget for Christopher. This will mean that an agreed amount will be paid into a special bank account each month and that we will then be responsible for paying all of our son's bills, including his care. We actually applied some two months ago, have been told it is on the way but in reality, as is the case with any Local Authority one has to wait for ever and a day to get things made official, to agree how much the budget might be for Chris.

Some of the things Carers will be responsible for will be to help Christopher with his daily chores, cleaning, laundry, ironing, cooking, making his bed and helping to put together a shopping list and then take him to the shop, or perhaps order online and have everything delivered initially. With regard to his finances, we will be taking care of those, supplying Chris and the Carers with enough cash that they need on a daily or weekly basis. I say cash but another thought is to use a Master Card, on which we can load a set figure as we feel is required.

Together with the Carers, we want to ensure that Christopher does not lead a life as a recluse. We want him to meet his neighbours, some of whom will welcome him to the area, others that may be a little sceptic. We will encourage Chris to go to any community gatherings that we think he can handle and enjoy.

Something else that Supported Living will offer is the opportunity to possibly take part in some voluntary work, perhaps on a farm. We know of several farms in our area that offer that chance to the members of society that would otherwise have little or nothing to look forward to and where Chris could attend a couple of times each week.

We are also hoping that we can arrange for Christopher to attend a local college. Work will have to be done to sort out what would be best for him, but we are confident there is something that he would enjoy.

As we live in our own homes, I guess something we all enjoy is how we decorate our home, what colours we like best. So far through his life, Christopher has had to accept what he has been given, or what colours his room had been painted. We want supported living to give him that very important choice, for him to decide what his home looks like. I suppose the big thing about supported living and I cannot repeat it enough is giving our son, the freedom of choice. I keep mentioning choice, but I make no apology, it is such an important thing in all of our lives. Carrying out as many things as possible and to empower him within his own home, his familiar surroundings.

Perhaps at this point a word of advice, if you are now thinking about supported living for your son or daughter and it's something we had to take on board is that when searching for an appropriate home it must always have an extra bedroom. That's a bedroom for the carer that will in most cases sleep over to ensure the safety of your child at night.

Before ending this chapter, I want to assure you, that if you are thinking about supported living but worried about it, that there is plenty of help and advice available. However, something you will always have to work with, and I hope yours is more co-operative than ours has been, is the local authority and ICB in your area.

It is not the local authority that is necessarily at fault, it is some of the individuals within the system that can be the problem. Those that think they are above you, that think they should make all of the decisions, to talk down to you. Do not let that worry you. You and your child both have rights.

Perhaps my most important piece of advice if you live in the United Kingdom and you are in a similar situation to us is that you apply for Deputyships for your child that has special needs and lacks capacity. It is always best to apply for both, the Health and Welfare Deputyship and the one for Property and Finance. That is again something I have mentioned earlier but have repeated it because of its importance.

At least with these secured you are able to have more say in what happens with your child's future. If you are not confident to complete the application yourself as we did, look for a solicitor that offers reasonable rates. To be honest if you take your time, read all of the notes and you are fairly well educated I am sure you could complete the forms yourself. Incidentally all of the forms are available online from the Office of The Public Guardian. Go for it and good luck.

CHAPTER 26

Fighting Chrissy's Cause

This chapter is probably the most difficult to write. Earlier in the book I made you aware of how Christopher was abused and neglected, mostly in the back end of 2021.

Before the incidents that highlighted the problems, we would face from November 2021 to present, life had not been brilliant for our son at the residential home but was just about bearable.

Since the quality of the home was put into question life has been very difficult indeed both for our son and for us as parents and his deputies. There have been days when one would have thought that it was us under investigation, that we were the guilty parties, but I gather from the Solicitor helping us with this that it can be a ploy to perhaps change and possibly meddle with our thoughts.

At this moment in time, I can assure you that nothing will change my mind, nor I believe that of my wife. We have lived through many days filled with our tears, having had to witness so many dark moments for Chris. The pain and the psychological injuries, both on Christopher and us, will never be known other than the impression the specialist doctors will form over their investigation period.

We can and have tried to imagine the physical injuries and the pain they caused to our son but in reality, it is only Christopher, with limited verbal ability that could possibly bring the true reality to light. That is why a top and very experienced psychologist is being brought in to study Chris and report his findings back in time for the court proceedings.

As already said, we have an excellent legal team that will, we are confident, fight to the bitter end if they have to and achieve what Chris deserves, justice. It is however for that reason that I cannot and will not jeopardise this case by saying too much more at this stage. It is a case of being patient, to let our legal representatives do their job and for us, as parents, for the time being to stay quiet, to continue to be there for Christopher and to seriously start looking for his new home.

With a new home, new fully experienced carers and a good plan I am sure that we can offer Chris a great future. We have spent the last twenty-three years battling for improvement, for fairness and for everything that is just. It has been difficult, and we could have easily ducked out on some occasions, but we have always been parents that will without hesitation fight a just cause, whether it be for Christopher or any other member of our family.

A friend recently said to me, "It will all work out Charles, you are born fighters". We are fighters but not may I hastily add physical fighters. It is important to remember that words will often last much longer and have much more affect than the pain you may inflict on someone by becoming physical. Have your facts ready, stay calm and deliver your words with passion, that is my advice, although I must admit it has been very difficult to honour my own advice at times.

We can only hope, pray and keep going to the bitter end, making sure our son has a future that he can enjoy and feel free to make choices that he wants and so deserves.

CHAPTER 27

Walk a While in My Shoes

Throughout this book as in my first I am trying to tell you as much as I can about the different schools that our son attended, the problems that needed dealing with and looking to find a way forward. None of it is easy for my wife or me.

Perhaps what I haven't told you enough about is what it's like for us. That's why I thought I should invite you, just for a while, to walk in my shoes.

There is one thing I can share right away and that is the endless stress that both Tina and I suffer every day. Much of that stress is caused by bureaucracy, people from the ICB, the Local Authority and many others that we have to take on with a view to getting what is best for our beloved son.

There is one thing for sure and that is if we were not prepared to fight our son's cause every day he would get very little in the way of support and no meaningful progress would be made. Right now, following his current home neglecting and abusing him we find ourselves, whilst trying to find a new home, in a constant battle over funding, in particular the personal health budget. It would appear that the case manager and her seniors would be quite content to approve a budget based on a minimum wage structure. That would mean agency staff, just in off the street would be expected to care for our severely autistic son, his challenging behaviours, his complicated life and much more. That is exactly the reason why the neglect and abuse happened at his residential home in November 2021. Anti-Psychotic Medication missed for twenty-two days and failure to call in a doctor for over seventy-two hours in relation to an arm injury that almost ended up as Sepsis.

You know, when I try to get to sleep at night and I know Tina is the same, it's a real struggle to accept another day is over, that I have done my best and that I should be able to take the rest I deserve. It just does not work like that. We lay there, wondering what will come up tomorrow. Will for instance, Chris self-harm? That's often brought on by a behaviour that is used, in place of speech by our son and many others that have problems speaking. What is he is asking for when he takes to a behaviour? He may be able to talk but it does not mean he is able to hold a proper conversation. We are very often second guessing what might happen next. Whilst Tina and I are well aware of what clues to look for, others are not and before they realise there's a problem it is too late.

This is what worries us with the ICB wanting to employ inexperienced staff at £11 an hour. Would they be able to detect and control a serious behaviour. Are people with very little training, perhaps having signed on at an agency for the first time and never worked in an autistic setting before, really capable of keeping Christopher safe? Minimum wage! Is that really what is needed? Many people of that standing are interested in one thing usually. Their pay packet at the end of the month and judging by the home Chris is currently at they do not ensure those agency staff have sufficient training.

Since the abuse and neglect episode Chris has been cared for by very experienced staff, grade 5 nurses and yet the Local Authority are more than happy to take a step back and mess up everything these wonderful nurses have done thus far.

There is never a night that passes without we lay there, chatting about what has happened, what might happen or what we are waiting for the ICB or the local authority to sort out. Without doubt, the most frustrating thing that we have to deal with is the procrastination that the authorities seem to be so good at. I think many of them may have gone to the same place that trains our politicians, always an answer but never the one you want to hear, often just another question.

What none of you will probably be aware of is that when we have finished our late-night board meeting discussing Chris and his needs, we then have to turn to trying to plan what we will do the next morning that will contribute towards building our business. Yes, we have our own business, working with essential oils, and sharing our knowledge with people from many countries around the world. Our oils, being the only 100% pure certified oils of any repute are wanted by so many and it's not just a case of selling them a bottle of oil, they need to know the benefits and how to use the oil wisely.

We, that is us and many others connected to the company run classes every day of the week, lasting an hour on zoom with as many as 40 or 50 joining the class from countries as far away as America, Australia, South Africa and even our newest country India. There are over 130 countries that we operate in, to date.

One of the great attributes of these amazing oils is that they help us to stay calm, chilled, relaxed and even mostly free from pain. In fact, we use some of them on Christopher and they have the most calming effect.

Having found the oils are so beneficial to both of our sons, we have started doing online presentations in order that we can spread the word and help others. The oils used correctly have brought Chris down from what potentially could be another bad incident.

I have a confession to make. During the last eighteen months, such has been our need to dedicate time to our son, our business has suffered badly. The people I mentioned earlier, those that sit in offices and make decisions about Chris, they get paid whether they turn up or not. Here is a clear difference, if we don't work, we don't expand our business and that of course affects our income. That is our choice of course and I, unlike some perhaps have no problem when I have to choose between by business and my flesh and blood. It has always been and will always remain that my son and my family come first.

So finally, with a Good Night My Love and God Bless to Tina, I turn over and do my best to grab some sleep before something else starts activating in my grey matter. That happens, oh so often, it might mean another hour or two working on something in my mind but by now I do my best not to disturb my dear wife. She needs all the sleep she can get. With Fibromyalgia plaguing her, she is so often exhausted. I am so proud of her, how she works so hard during the day, the housework, our business and taking care of anything that needs sorting for Christopher and the rest of the family.

Perhaps it's a good thing some mornings that we do oversleep, a bonus if you like but with Chris in care, albeit somewhere that we don't want him to be at the moment at least we can take our time getting through breakfast, before cracking on with everything that is on the radar.

So much of our lives revolve around what we have to do for Chris and the family. Christopher's brother, Charlie, has enough problems for sure. There is no doubt in our minds that he too is on the spectrum. Twice he has been diagnosed with doctors absolutely certain he has autism, maybe just asperges but by the end of the tests they told us no.

We knew it was enough that he does definitely have acute anxiety and a slow transiting bowel, poor chap. Now twenty-five, Charlie is still a real concern, but he is what he is; he is a lovely young man and all we do is offer our support when he feels it is needed.

Somehow, I think Charlie does understand why we must spend so much time looking after his brother, especially during the period of his life that has caused so much concern. Some of my story is still to come of course but as I get through the journey you will realise that each and every one of the family has had real need for concern for both of the boys.

Out of total coincidence Tina has today, yes, as I write, taken Charlie to see the Doctor and guess what we found out. The Doctor told us that it is written into Charlie's notes that on the second assessment that took place in 2008 he was in fact diagnosed with Aspergers Syndrome. Why were we not told at the time. Had Charlie not moved to a new surgery after his Art Course at University we may never have known. Our old Doctors had never mentioned this to us. I mean, how many of us ask to go through their own medical records.

We used to visit Christopher once a week, on a Wednesday afternoon and that has been his time for years and he knows it. Suddenly, as Covid rampaged the Country, indeed the World and with lockdown in place, we could only stay in touch by using zoom. Zoom, something before Covid that was not too well known but now it is a household name. We have used it for several years to talk with people all over the world about the oils and found it such a blessing during the darkest moments where everyone was forced to stay at home. How though, do you explain covid to someone like Chris, it was so painful having to keep saying, won't be long now Chris, the bug will be gone soon. Then mummy and daddy can visit you and we can have great big hugs.

All you could do was hope what you had told him had some element of truth, he was clearly missing us, in fact almost pining according to his carers. Thank God, with some relief from the pandemic we were again allowed to visit in the flesh, albeit a case of meeting outside and wrapped up in what made us look as if we were "Clingfilm Mummies".

As you read through the remaining chapters you will find it was necessary to increase our visits to twice each week, visiting still on a Wednesday but also on a Sunday. Christopher loves every visit because with each and every one he knows he can demand his drive to MacDonalds. Now and again, choosing the chicken factory for a change, you know where I mean, where most things come in buckets. I think we discovered why Chris liked going out to grab a takeaway. The food at the home was of poor quality and plenty of it quickly found its way to the bin, once our boy had rescued what he felt was edible.

You see, even things like worrying about if he was getting enough to eat would add to the stress that we had to endure. Even on days when you don't really feel up to doing that one-hundred-mile round trip, you know you have to, it's your duty, your son will be waiting, and you cannot afford to let him down. If we were to discount the Covid lockdown period and the occasional holiday I reckon we could count on maybe two hands the times we have missed visiting Chris. Whether we were happy with where he was being looked after or not there was no question of letting our son down. Think about this, who, when you know there is such a loving young person waiting for you, almost depending on you, would want to break his heart.

I told you earlier in the book about the happiest place that Chris was at, the most amazing school one could ever wish for, and it was whilst Chris was there that I sprung that surprise on Tina. Charlie was at an age where he was happy for his mum and dad to take a break, he did not want to join us, independence creeping in you see. I cannot tell you enough how special a mum Tina has been and still is to both boys and my older kids from a previous marriage and some grandkids. A mum that deserved something very special. I had been saving without saying too much and had worked out that I had just about reached the figure I needed.

"Tina", I said one evening, "Where's the place I have always said I would like to visit". She couldn't think straight and tried unsuccessfully to come up with a few suggestions. Then it dawned on her, "Australia", she said, "How can we afford to go there"? "Yep", I replied, "Your right and we are going". I explained how I had been saving for ages and this holiday was to say a great big thank you to her, for everything she had done for all of us. I think, well I know it took a while to sink in. I had been talking to a company that took care of everything for you. Just tell them what you want, where you want to go and when and leave the worrying behind. I had the brochure already and we spent the next couple of weeks working out all the details, ensuring we stayed within our budget. A month down under, it would be amazing, but we had to make sure Chris was ok with it all.

Hopefully, you have worked out a little of how we have coped over the years, there have been plenty of tears that's for sure but there have also been lots of laughter and fun and that's what is really important.

A person that can smile in the face of adversity has a chance in life. We could easily have let things drive us under, we are still under pressure as I write but we will never give in. Never will we let people who think they might be higher up the social ladder than us, that think they have the right to dominate mine and my family's lives be allowed to get away with that. From this you may have confirmation that social snobbery is my biggest hate. We are all born into this world equal, will leave equal and whilst on mother earth we all deserve to be treated with great respect and that includes those that through no fault of their own were born with or grew into a disability. In fact, we, the unafflicted should show more love, more understanding and our aim in life should be to help all of those that have serious problems, to feel that love and care in abundance. No one is just a number!

I do hope you have enjoyed walking along, listening to me bring up some problems, some hardships and some of how our wonderful young son has been a good reason to keep us busy and out of trouble.

Christmas just as COVID-19 started to leave us.

April 2023 - Chris striding out, part of his 568,000 Steps for Autism.

CHAPTER 28

The Best Way To Buy

The information I am about to share shocked Tina and me when we first heard about it. Our severely autistic son, to buy his home, how could that be possible.

Once we heard about supported living as an option our first question that we asked the authorities was, "Why had we not been told of this option before?" Why, when it is so difficult to find suitable Residential Homes, these days was Supported Living kept under wraps?

After all, we have since found out that it is something that the UK government is apparently encouraging. We started to ask around for answers. I started to search the internet for anyone or any company that may be able to help.

I sent lots of messages out and looked forward to the replies. I have to say, there were only a few in my search that did not bother replying. Some replied with positive information and asking us for more details. Others replied telling us that supported living was not something that they were doing at this moment in time.

Have you ever tried finding something and you come up with more than you expected. What's the saying, "You fell on your feet". Surprise, surprise, that is exactly what happened to me. I received a reply from a lady who has spent many of her years working voluntarily to help others with disabilities to find somewhere suitable to live.

It was indeed an extreme pleasure to have my first conversation with this very special lady wherein she explained how she had first helped a lady with mental health problems, purchase her own home some twenty-six years ago, back in 1996, I make that. I now know that this lady, she deserves a title in my opinion, saved the young disabled person being placed in a mental hospital, her last option before the intervention of Jayne.

Jayne has set up and registered a charity called Rightful Housing. She is a very well-educated person, passionate to help others and was the one that set up a system, now known as HOLD. The system allowed the young lady with mental health issues to purchase her own home under a shared ownership idea, whereby her side of the mortgage would be paid by the DWP, the Department of Works and Pension. It would be an interest only mortgage.

I am so delighted to tell you that the young lady that Jayne helped, still lives happily in that same home. How amazing that someone's life could be turned around by someone that truly cared about others. Incidentally, Jayne has spent many years now helping others, that without her input would have struggled. I make no secret that if I had not been lucky on the day, I spent searching the internet I would almost certainly not have made the progress that has been made to find Christopher his forever home, that is if everything went right from here on.

Jayne offers another special attribute that I definitely need at times. At some meetings with the authorities and because of their procrastination my passion will start to take over. Jayne will step in and calm the situation, for which I am truly grateful.

Jayne's achievement, those twenty-six years back was reported in the Financial Times, and she received an invitation to attend the House of Lords, to be recognised for her amazing work. A young businessman, named David, spotted the report in the Financial Times and was eager to help Jayne in her mission to help others. In the shell of a nut, what happened was David set up a mortgage company, My Safe Home, specifically designed to help disabled people purchase their own home. David, being another very special person, is someone like Jayne, just wanting to help others that are less able. To date between them Jayne and David, together with another company that has become involved have helped over one thousand less advantaged people use the HOLD system, enabling them to own their own homes and have security for the rest of their lives.

It is people like Jayne and David that do indeed deserve to be recognised. Devoting much of their lives to help others. I know Jayne works tirelessly in other areas, still with the aim of helping those that need it most and from what I gather never counting the cost. Tina and I will be forever grateful for the help we have received thus far and for what we will continue to receive. I know that if Christopher were able, he too would personally and wholeheartedly thank them for their time and kindness.

What worries me most is when I ask myself the question, where would we be in the United Kingdom without Jayne and David and the many more out there doing similar work. Is there enough encouragement for more people to help within the field of housing for disabled people.

Should our government be making more of encouraging those with mental and physical health problems, or their legal representatives to take a closer look at Supported Living.

One of the issues we have personally found and that we need to sort out and I am sure is a problem to many more is the ability to raise the deposit required. Whilst the Department of Works and Pensions are prepared to pay the mortgage, repayable of course when the property is eventually sold or if a person passes on, they are unable to help with the deposit.

We have heard that many CCG's or Local Authorities around the country have loaned the deposit to the person wishing to purchase. It is not a risk as it is written into a legal document, as is any other mortgage and again repayable if the property is sold or if the person passes on. This at the moment, is our stumbling block, our Local Authority are refusing to help, using a number of excuses.

Right at this moment we are working hard to find another avenue that may be able to help us unless of course the Local Authority decides to change its mind. Something I have been advised to do by an officer at the Office of the Public Guardian is to write to the local Health Ombudsman and as many other people in positions that may be able to put pressure on the right people or departments. Once we have secured the deposit for Christopher's mortgage we can move ahead, look for suitable properties and get the legal work started.

One thing you will need is legal permission to purchase a property on your child's behalf. If you are not yet deputies, then I advise you to get that process under way, ensuring that the judge gives you the necessary legal rights to purchase, that's in section 2a of the Property and Finance document. If you already hold a deputyship, make sure the right to purchase is included and if not make an urgent application for that rite to be added. All of this takes time, and one cannot afford to take your foot off the gas.

Another way of raising a deposit that has been suggested to Tina and I is through a charity, if one exists that will offer such help. I am currently searching diligently in the hope that we can come across some help and will of course let you know if we have been lucky before I close the back cover on this story.

Since the person that used to represent the CCG and worked closely with us mysteriously disappeared and her replacement being far from helpful came on the scene it has been extremely difficult to get any support, anything we want to know or do is basically down to us.

People that trifle with the truth really annoy me but when someone in a position like the current Case manager holds back information and then trifles with the truth to try and belittle Tina and I, or to get their own way it absolutely infuriates me. Having taken advice, I am very close to exposing some of this to the media, I believe the world deserves to know about people like this. They are dangerous. I think they are like it as they believe getting their own way will prove something to their superiors. I have other ideas.

Maybe before I complete my story there will be a fairy tale ending. Perhaps, if an editor gets wind of the problem, we are having they might well like to know more. That's fine by me but they will not get it for nothing if you get my meaning.

Let me say, that even if we are unable to find the deposit for our son's home, we still have another road to go down. We will, in fact already are looking at the possibility of securing a property with a Life Long Assured Tenancy. That is as good as buying a property, it just means that you cannot sell it. It will give our son the security we are so desperate for him to have, although all he is doing is renting on a long-term tenancy.

Life and the way things happen can be very strange, as one door closes sometimes another door opens. This is exactly what has happened. One moment we are experiencing disappointment and the next have something else to look forward to. There has been an amazing development in the hunt for our son's forever home. A lady that works in the housing department at the local authority, specifically looking after the interest of young disabled adults contacted us to ask if we would be interested in looking at a bungalow they had recently purchased. In fact, they had bought two bungalows and we could choose between the two. Each of the large bungalows is to be gutted, divided into two and purpose built for a specific person.

After the disappointment we suffered, we were lifted out of that hole and now look forward to Chris having his own bungalow on a long-term lease. We are working with the Housing Association and the Architect to give Christopher whatever we believe would be best for him. How amazing is that!

BUT, and another but. The CCG are still trying to have their own way. With a personal Health Budget we are supposed to be able to employ carers of our choice, but we are being held up. We have sought an excellent company, but the local authority has other ideas. Let me make that clearer. The case manager, who should be helping us, has decided she will not help the company of our choice. They want a care company that pays just a minimum wage and employs many inexperienced agency staff.

They are again placing our son in danger. Have they not recognised how Chris regressed before the introduction of Thornbury. He is a very complex young man and needs care to suit that complexity. Money, some say is the problem.

Rest assured we will not give up on our son's future, we will battle on.

CHAPTER 29

I've Walked a Hundred Miles

Since the end of October 2021, when Christopher was neglected and abused at his care home I have walked, with my dear wife, a hundred miles, as the saying goes, in search of a home that would be able to look after our son safely and give him much more freedom of choice.

Choice, probably the most important thing that anyone of us can look for in our lives. Without choice we become prisoners within our own homes, within our own systems. We all must and all deserve the right to choose and also if we want to the right to change.

I suppose the most contentious choice in a residential care home is what we want to eat. Christopher for the last five years now has had little or no choice. I can say five years without doubt, the five years being up in two weeks' time, the 20th August 2023 from the date when he transitioned from his amazing school into this residential home. A home we are working so hard to get him out of and into something so much better.

Since October 2021 my wife and I have searched through and visited so many residential homes. Travelled miles, with our original CCG Commissioner and also sometimes one of Christopher's previous Social Workers, who was so hard working, understanding and kind, working with us right up to her last thirty minutes in the job.

Some Homes have looked better than others, but they all appear to have one common factor. That Choice is not freely available. It is for that reason that we have turned away from residential homes and now looking for supported living. I am not saying that the carers at some homes do not want the residents to have choice, it is their management team that dictates how the home is run.

I truly believe that much of it comes down to money. Finance rules so many things today. As with many businesses, and a care home is unfortunately a business, often with little feeling for whom they supposedly care, the man at the top wants the most and gets the most, whilst those working on the shop floor are paid a pittance for what they have to do. Good carers spend so much time learning, and training and they are invaluable. I'm going to stick my neck out here a little and say that if the man at the top wants plenty, then that has to come at a cost to others and that is why many carers earn little more than a minimum wage. It is so sad and hardly surprising that they don't feel up to doing any more than they have to. When that sort of thing happens the care industry suffers as the staff that are good at their job, are shown little appreciation and move on elsewhere, often to something completely new.

One thing is so terribly important, and all so often gets overlooked by local authorities, the ICB and the like. They appear to think that all residents are the same, that none of them need more care than the next man or lady. You see it is the job of those working within a local authority to save money wherever they can, no matter how that might affect residents. That is the very problem with our son. He is right up at the top of the autistic spectrum. Coupled with his challenging behaviour and ADHD and his Sensory Processing disorder he is a real handful. Does that matter to the authority, do they not recognise some are different. No, I believe they tar most with the same brush and if they get their own way will be quite happy to pay just the minimum wage to carers, perhaps in the hope that they may score a few extra Brownie points, show their boss they are worthy of a good pay increase. Adopting this attitude is far from fair. I do also believe and have now seen evidence that some people within the system always have to be right, no matter if they are or not and no matter what pain that causes others.

It's not fair on the resident and not fair on those that work as carers. Asking inexperienced carers to work with autism is bad enough but to throw them headfirst with severe autism is criminal in my mind. You know, I remember my dear old dad saying to me on a number of occasions when we were talking about getting the best person for a job. Take your time, look for the person that shines and be fair with them. He then went on to say, remember son, if you pay peanuts, you are likely to get ……. I'll leave you to work that out.

Just to prove that this does happen here is a true case of someone not knowing anything about caring. Yes, it happened on the day our son arrived at his residential care home, where the neglect and abuse took place. The first guy to work with Chris had no experience of care let alone autism and the registered manager put him with our son, being shadowed by someone who was not there much of the time. I know, what you're thinking, you have mentioned this before. Yes, I have but it's important.

In that person's defence he got to know us well and asked us many questions about Chris and about how he could best help him. To his credit, having left that home after a couple of years he is now qualified and a manager within a company that offers supported living. We remain great friends and he never talks with us without asking after Christopher.

Just for a moment though, let me bring you what I think is wrong with most residential homes. It comes back to the freedom of choice and probably the choice that is lacking in most homes is the choice of what food a resident wants to eat and of course when they want to eat it. Christopher has, if you like, two choices. Whether he eats the food put in front of him or he puts it in the bin.

During our search covering well over a year we have only found one or two homes that offer any real sort of choice, regarding food. The problem with choice usually relates to cost. The more choices on offer, the greater the cost and possibly there's a slight increase in waste, which I believe could be dealt with quite easily.

One home that we visited and where we had high hopes of Chris being accepted into had the choice of food sorted. They met with the six residents once a week and using very explicit picturesque menus chose the two most popular meals for each of the seven days ahead and both of those would be available on the designated days. Now to the waste. Staff at that home ate with the residents but were not allowed to choose what they wanted until the residents had decided what they were going to eat. That meant that staff got to eat what would otherwise be thrown away. None of them minded that because their meals were provided free of charge.

At the home where Chris has been for these last five years, choice of what food he could have and indeed the other residents, has been severely restricted. It was not until Tina and me complained about choice that the home produced a menu. It was only a written menu, so bear in mind and we think we are correct that our son is the only resident that can read, how do the others know what's on the menu.

Again, we complained and at last a picture menu appeared, but please don't get too excited. The pictures are small and extremely difficult to make out what is meant to depicted.

May I ask you a question? When have you gone out to eat, asked for a menu and shock, horror, there has only been one choice. I have always believed a menu needed to have at least two choices, otherwise what is the purpose of it.

One Sunday recently, when Chris was expecting the usual Sunday Roast, he was actually served a plate of boiled pasta with some garden peas mixed in with it, not even a creamy sauce to make the meal more appetising. I know I have mentioned this before but, in my mind, it is worth emphasizing how many residents at so many care homes are treated. A lovely roast meal that. Chris soon dispatched it but not in his stomach, it went in the bin. Now, I calculated that meal, served to the six residents would have cost no more than £5 sterling at a maximum. More evidence that the residents are not treated properly, not given a choice and not given what I consider nourishing food.

One of the other restrictions at many homes, because that is what a lack of choice actually means, residents are restricted, is the choice to do what you want and when you want. Does the resident want to go out? Sorry they cannot do that as there is no transport. I hope you understand what I mean? You will have to wait till tomorrow, another answer often given to my son. All sorts of excuses are given that take away the residents' choice. Sorry we can't take Chris swimming as we have no driver available is something our son has often had to endure.

Any care home has to be very careful about taking away choice and liberty in the United Kingdom, but it would seem the law is brushed aside on many occasions.

I honestly believe that carers working at the majority of residential care homes are under so much pressure from the management to cut costs wherever and whenever they can. Yet, what the home is paid for looking after each resident is massive. I have no objection for paying the cost for anything I choose to buy, providing I get value for money. In the care industry that is always something that is in question. Of course, many of the Local Authorities do not want to pay any more than they have to for the care of a resident. It is perhaps a bit of a vicious circle. Residents are, however, human beings and deserve to be treated with the same respect as those that own the care home. I cannot for the life of me see the difference.

I remember well, when I was a driving instructor, and I was picking up my next pupil from the care home she worked at. The lesson was at 3pm on a Sunday, roast dinner day for many and I will never forget how upset my lady was as she got into the car, she was crying her heart out. I gave her plenty of time to calm down and then asked what had upset her. She was one of the most caring persons you could wish to meet, and she told me that she had just witnessed the eleven elderly residents had just been fed using a chicken that weighed just three pounds. She vowed to report the home and only worked out her notice rather than leave immediately so she could be on duty when a surprise inspection took place. Having settled my pupil down we went for a lovely drive out and at the end she was delighted when I never charged her. She deserved that. It was in fact my last lesson of the day and I made my way home for my Sunday roast, a chicken weighing at least five pounds and shared by me and four of my family.

Perhaps now you can start to understand why residential homes are definitely not in our opinion suitable for Christopher, we need to be able to give him his life back, to give him CHOICE. Choice of everything in his life.

We are now continuing to do everything necessary to secure the bungalow that I mentioned earlier. With the idea of buying missed, Christopher's bungalow with be secured by a long-term tenancy.

Over the time of our search, we made suggestions that we believed could very quickly resolve the problem of finding a new home for our son but because it was me or my wife that came up with the idea, even though we are legal deputies for Chris, the Local Authority always found something wrong. These people are employees within a care system, there to help families not just the individual. However, it would seem they must have the last word. I think some have the idea that because they are a manager at the Local Authority, that they are above you, what they say goes. Even when you prove that members of staff are trifling with the truth to make themselves the one with all the power, their managers would seem to turn a blind eye. That is not just my feeling, I have evidence of that type of behaviour.

Please, always be careful, keep good records and don't be pushed around. That is why in an earlier chapter I emphasised the benefit of becoming a Legal Deputy. I cannot yet go into details, but I know for sure that a senior manager from the CCG tried to fix it so that Christopher stayed at the very home that had abused him, with the same manager and staff. This was all behind our backs and the woman concerned does not, as I write, know that we are aware she tried this. Rest assured she will do at the right time and so will her superiors and the law makers. Yes, Christopher is still at that same home, but we are now doing everything we can to move him into his own bespoke forever home.

No matter how many miles we have travelled in our search, some in the car others online we will continue to keep searching for the right house or bungalow and use the Supported Living principle for our Chris.

I will always flatly refuse to be pushed around, to be dictated to and to ensure that never happens as I have kept a few things up my sleeve that would, if shared be very shocking for you the public to read and very damaging for some of the so-called Gods, that work within the care system. I'm sure these people like to treat you like mere minnows in a pond whilst they are the sharks, always on top and doing you and your beloved child a favour.

Something that these sharks, and so many more will not have picked up on is the change in Christopher from when he arrived at this home to how he is now. When Chris left Hill House, he was a happy, bouncy young man, full of energy. Today and times I look back on during the five years at the residential home, he has often become unhappy, depressed, for which he has been medicated, and he has had to lean on his negative and challenging behaviours in order to communicate his frustration.

I sincerely hope that what I consider to be an honest assessment shared in this chapter has given every parent that cares for a child with special needs something to take away that will help them.

I must make it clear that both my wife and I have visited some amazing care homes during our search. Of course, that is the problem, if they are any good, they are very unlikely to have any vacancies. God Bless them, for being caring, honest and open in their approach to caring for those who are in need.

The wonderful thing is that after all of our travelling, much of it virtually, some actually on the road, that at last we are starting to see light at the end of the tunnel.

CHAPTER 30

Some Very Special People – Some Special Memories

I think it would be wrong of me if I did not recognise some of the people that have played a very special part in Christopher's life before I finish what I consider be a very special true-life story. Of the people I am paying special recognition to there is no particular order for they all, in their own way have been special to my son, angels if you like, always there to help whenever they have been needed. They have all helped to bring about some semblance of order in a life that has been very special and even certainly extraordinary in many people's minds. Some would have seen elements of Chris's life very sad but as parents we have battled hard and long to make sure at the end of the day it is the good things, the kind people that are remembered.

Some of those mentioned have known Chris, Tina and me for many years, whilst others have made an impact, even changed our son's life in a relatively short period of time, maybe as little as one or two years.

Rosie – Christopher's first and only teacher whilst he was at Ridgeway Way House school. To this day, Chris mentions Rosie. She was so devoted to her class but appeared to have a special affinity with Christopher. Patience was her virtue, for sure and with it helped to develop Chris from someone that needed so much when he first attended, to a young boy that started to ooze confidence and had started to use some simple words in his vocabulary. It was so sad when Rosie decided to retire. It was at that time we felt we needed to look for a school that specialised in autism but will always be grateful to Rosie for her dedication. She was a lady that always respected us and never failed to give one hundred percent of her best.

Julie – A Carer with Smile.   When Chris was a whole lot younger and was home at weekends, we were fortunate enough to be given a couple of hours each Sunday afternoon as a respite period. We were a little apprehensive waiting that first week for a carer to arrive, but we need not have worried at all. A tap at the door and it was a young lady named Julie who was to be our son's lead carer, accompanied by another person as Chris was two to one care when in the community. Chris was ready, shouting and screeching at the top of his voice and without any further ado was off with Julie to the car. Chris loved his two hours out with Julie, she was a mum herself and had all the finishing touches that a good mum always seems to have quite naturally. One week, when Julie arrived back home with Chris, something sparked him suddenly to pull Julie's hair. There was no doubt it hurt. Julie took it in her stride, not making a fuss and what's more was back at our door the following week, bang on time.

In fact, when Chris started to stay over at school on some weekends, Julie, took time to build up a rapport with our other son, who too had mental health problems. Julie spoke with her office, and it was decided she would take Charlie out when his brother wasn't needing her. She found out that Charlie was into wildlife and decided to take him to Marwell Zoo, just a few miles from where we live. It didn't finish there as one week Julie arrived with an Ostrich egg, blown of course. It turned out that she knew some of the people at the zoo and they gave her the egg for Charlie. Some guys go that extra mile and Julie was certainly one of those. Incidentally the Ostrich egg still proudly sits in our lounge, resting in a rather large vase. Thank you, Julie, for all of your dedicated time and patience.

John – Another carer from smile.

John, was indeed yet another amazing person who worked for the same care company as Julie called and looked after Christopher when Julie was not available. Julie could not make every week because of her family commitments so when she was off John would be there to keep the continuity going for Chris. Having familiar faces was important and John was another person that Chris learned to trust and respect. John had come to England from Nigeria, where he was a Head Teacher in a senior school. He had so many wonderful attributes but at that time did not have the qualifications required over here to continue teaching. Hopefully, not having seen him now for a while he may well have the qualifications needed and may be teaching again.

On arrival in England, John found a job with Smile and I for one was so pleased he had done so. John was amazing with Chris. Some days, when John was the only carer, I had to go out with him to make up the two to one. I have to tell you; it was not just a pleasure but an honour to be able to learn from this man. The way he spoke so calmly to Chris and how he dealt with any behaviour issues was outstanding. Thank you, John, for caring for Christopher and for teaching me so much. I am a firm believer that no matter how much you think you know, there is still room to learn more and to improve in everything you do in life. John, it was always a pleasure to be in your company!

Simon – One of Thornbury's best. Simon was sent to help us look after Chris when our son was around fifteen years old. It was the summer holidays and Chris had been expelled from the school in Dorset. For what reason, we shall never know but let me say it was a blessing in disguise. It meant that after the holiday Chris would start five years of amazing schooling at Hill House School.

Now back to Simon who spent nearly every day of the six weeks holiday helping us look after, what was then, a very difficult young man. Yet by the end of the holiday break Chris had started to change, to calm down, to have far less negative behaviours and thanks mostly to the care he received from Simon. Not only did he help Chris, but he taught us so much that has over the years been so useful. We are still friends with Simon today and his name is often spoken by Chris. It was not too long back when Simon, now with a different company was asked to conduct an assessment on Christopher at his care home. Wow! When Simon went through the door and Chris immediately recognised him, it was hugs all round. Thank you, Simon, for the impression that you left on our son.

Fran – Christopher's current Senior Occupational Therapist

Special, Amazing, Outstanding. I cannot find enough powerful adjectives to describe Fran. At the start of helping Chris her back was to the wall, for she had been told by the manager at the residential care home that Chris was fine and did not need any help. As soon as Fran was made aware that her intervention was in fact urgently required, she jumped into the breach, as the saying goes and has been helping Chris since on a fairly regular basis. Fran advised us that Chris needed specialist equipment and to avoid delays delivered what she would normally hold as her test equipment to the home within days making it clear that it was only a temporary arrangement.

She asked the local authority to fund new equipment that included a Peanut ball, but it was like trying to get blood from a stone. It took several months for the local authority to make up their mind whose budget would be used to pay for the much-needed items. Has Fran ever panicked? No, not at all, her equipment remained with Chris until the new order eventually arrived.

Fran is thorough to say the least. Recently, working with us as parents, she completed an eighteen-page report, a very detailed sensory diet. When she visits Chris, and she does so as often as possible, it is never a fleeting visit, spending several hours with our son, constantly assessing him and helping him. Both Tina and I wonder where Chris would be without the dedication of this special lady.

Kate – Head Teacher at Christopher's very last school, Hill House and Vella a teaching assistant at Hill House School.

Kate, the head teacher that has not only helped our son but so many more that have passed through Hill House School whilst under her leadership. One of the most dedicated ladies you could ever wish to meet. So often arranging something out of the ordinary for everyone in her care. Bands brought into school to offer different types of music from around the world and Sports days that included the parents as well as the pupils. Kate would often turn up at the school of an evening or a weekend, having been to a local farm, laden with enough strawberries to feed an army.

Now, let me tell you how she helped Christopher in particular. She recognised our son was going through a difficult period in his last year at the school and that he needed some extra one to one care. Whilst the local authority was procrastinating about whether to pay for an additional person Kate found funding within her budget and Chris had the extra person required working with him for the remainder of that school year.

Incidentally, the person assigned to this roll had a new job waiting for him, but he would not move until Chris was safely transitioned to his adult placement. He too was a very special person whose name was Vella. I remember him saying to me, "I am not leaving here until our Chris is safely transitioned into his new home." How thoughtful is that. How many people do you know that would put someone else before their own future? This young man was indeed very special. Vella, we salute you!

Gaynor- Teacher at Hill House

Boy, was this lady special. Without doubt she was able to control our Chris better than anyone. She had so much respect for Chris, and it was reciprocal. Even when Chris decided to be a bit awkward or act up it only took a count from one to five by Gaynor and our son was back on track. I truly believe that no matter who it is, if they show respect to Christopher, they can get him to do almost anything. Such was the bond between this lovely lady and our son it became very difficult for both when it was time for them to part company when Chris moved to what we thought would be his for ever home.

Gaynor suggested that we get a full life size cardboard cutout of Chris and take it to his new home whilst the real Cheeky Chappie remained at Hill House. You know, I am pretty sure, that providing we kept up our visits to Hill House every Wednesday, Christopher would have been quite happy with that arrangement. What's more, if we had taken the cardboard cut out to the care home instead of Chris, I don't think some of the carers would have noticed.

Since Chris left Gaynor and Hill House, I have found out that Gaynor had actually moved on to another school herself, promotion I believe, although could it have been broken heart syndrome; was she worried that she would keep bumping into Chris around every corner at the school. If you ever read this Gaynor, please rest assured that your name is often on Christopher's tongue, you are one that he truly misses.

Jayne – An angel that appeared just at the right time.

How do you say, Out of The Blue! Jayne came along at the right moment for sure. It was a chance encounter with Jayne, bumping into her web site whilst online and having the courage to share our problem of Chris's housing with her when she responded. Such a knowledgeable lady and one that without, we would be truly struggling. This lady set up a scheme to help disabled people purchase their own homes. Twenty-Six years ago Jayne sprang into action to prevent a young lady being placed into a mental hospital. That young lady with Jayne's guidance bought her own home and still lives in it today. Incidentally the carer that started looking after her, still does and has actually moved in permanently.

The scheme is called HOLD, Jaynes company is called Rightful Housing and a young man joined her and set up a mortgage company, specifically again for disabled people, called My Safe Homes after reading in the Financial Times about Jayne and her visit to the House of Lords to be honoured for her achievement.

We are so lucking to now have Jayne supporting us, offering so much of her advice. We are so grateful to you Jayne and would love to see you and others I have mentioned acknowledged nationally for your achievements.

There is another lady that has become something extremely special to Christopher and I want to save that just for a little longer if I may. I will not forget because the lady I refer to has become unforgettable, almost family.

At this point I think it most important that I apologise to anyone who feels hurt by not being mentioned personally. The list could run into hundreds, and I want you to know that to each and every one that has been a special part of our son's life so far, we deeply appreciate you and everything you have done for our son.

You may be wondering how I am able to pick these very special people out from so many that have been a part of Christopher's life and indeed our lives.

I believe I have done it the right way. I have looked back at the whole of our son's life and decided that the people I have chosen have quite simply MADE A DIFFERENCE! If you like, it has been looking at Christopher's reactions towards certain people, that has helped me, I hope you understand.

Something else however came to my mind whilst writing this chapter. I have mentioned throughout the book about battles we have had with various authorities and how they have found it difficult to accept our opinions. Think of this please? All of these very special people I have mentioned have not just been special for our son, they have had their special influences on us as parents.

We have learnt so much from them and others that we feel we can to an extent, consider ourselves experts in the field of living with autism. Yet we are treated by those authoritarians as if we know nothing. Whilst many of those have sat in their offices making somewhat blind decisions, we have been there in the trenches, caring and battling for the benefit of our son and many others on the spectrum.

The dedication by us both to help our son cannot, I believe, be questioned. For instance, when Tina first heard about Chris being diagnosed with Sensory Processing Disorder, she did no more than to enrol on an official course, which she passed and now has a far better understanding. That is not just good parenting, it is someone that cares and someone that has a better knowledge in the field of autism.

CHAPTER 31

A Battle We Were Not Prepared to Lose

When we thought about Supported Living and buying Chris his own home we had to also think if we were to be responsible for his Personal Health Budget to think about finding the right Care Company to look after our son.

This is where we had a right battle with the new Case manager that had been appointed after her fantastic predecessor, having been put under pressure by her superiors had resigned.

We had been made aware by a very good friend, called Simon, who I mentioned in an earlier chapter, during his time with Thornbury Nurses that he was now associated with a new company since leaving Thornbury.

Simon, what a true gentleman he was, showing us so much respect as parents and imparting masses of his knowledge upon us during the six weeks he supported Christopher. We have remained in touch with him since that summer and in fact have become very good friends.

You see, with us pushing to get Christopher moved from the home that had so badly let him down, it was absolutely imperative that we find a care company that we could trust and one that had a first-class reputation.

We had in fact spoken to the owner of a care company in London, after being passed his details by another amazing person that got on so well with Chris when he worked with him at the residential home. Unfortunately, John, although hurt by leaving our son behind had no other option but to leave and find somewhere else to work, somewhere he would be appreciated.

John spoke with his boss, and he agreed to conduct an assessment on Christopher as soon as possible. Although Chris passed that assessment with flying colours, it was a disappointing outcome. Tony, the owner of the care company did everything he could to find a suitable property in or around Hayes, just outside the City. If he had found the right place, he was going to buy it and

Chris would have been moved there with his old carer John, looking after him again. It seemed it was just not meant to happen.

That was when we placed a post on our Facebook page, almost pleading with anyone who might know of a vacancy somewhere in the South of England for our son. At this time, we were still of the mind that we might get help with a deposit to purchase Chris his own home and therefore we would need to find the right carers and fast.

That was when Simon contacted us and told us he wanted to help. He told us all about Kind Tailored Care, based in the west of England and Wales and assured us that we must put our trust in the name, Kind, Tailored, Care. Three very special components that when brought together by their CEO, Sophie, meant there was indeed a specialist company that took their time to provide whatever was needed for each individual's care. They acknowledge that no two people requiring care are anywhere near the same and so they tailor according to the needs.

We did not rush into anything accept asked Simon and Sophie if they could conduct an assessment at their earliest convenience. On the day of the assessment in North Hampshire, both Simon and Sophie spent an appropriate amount of time with Christopher but not over the top. What was so special on that day was that Christopher remembered Simon as soon as he arrived and yet it had been around eight years since they last met. Christopher's first reaction was to say, "Simon a Hug".

Neither of these specialists from Kind Tailored Care were in a hurry to dash of back to the west country after they had bid farewell to Chris. They in fact met with us at the local just across the road from the care home, yes, a pub, where we enjoyed a working lunch and cokes all round, whilst we shared as much information as possible and answered numerous questions. With Christopher's history fairly fresh in Simon's mind he and Sophie were able to make a decision that they felt they could offer the specialist care that Chris needed. They had concluded that Christopher was still a very complex person and that his care should be appropriate to his needs. It would not be cheap, but we had seen what "Cheap Care" had done to our son in his current residential home.

The next step was to inform the case manager at the ICB that in our opinion we had found the right carers and to ask her to take the next steps to have Kind Tailored Care registered in Southampton. Of course, there were other matters that had to be checked but we felt confident. Kind Tailored Care were asked to submit their estimate of costs, and this is where everything started to fall apart.

So many of the professionals involved with our son were mind set on him needing more than just ordinary care and supported us along those lines. However, the ICB and the Local Authority were determined not to spend any more money than they had to and insisted another care company be asked to complete an assessment, a company they already knew would be cheaper.

Then it all went quiet. For over two months, we heard nothing. It is usual for any care company not to spend some of their time, whilst accessing someone to speaking to the parents; let's be honest they are the ones that know the most. Not having heard anything we decided to email the social worker and ask what was happening, how did the assessment go? The answer we got back, "Oh it went well!" That was it, not another word.

We were absolutely disgusted with the way we were being treated and decided to send an email to the company the Local Authority were banking on. It wasn't too long before we received a reply and a request to meet with us on zoom. What did it all mean? When we met, the company could not apologise enough, they thought we had been kept in the loop by the case manager and the social worker, but nothing was further from the truth. They had deliberately kept everything to themselves. When asked why, one of them said they were not sure we could deal with all the pressure. What a load of POPPICOT.

We were still in no doubt that we wanted Kind Tailored Care to be the ones that would look after our son, but the authorities would not stump up enough funds.

It was just about this time when something else happened that changed things again. We were contacted by a lady that works within Southampton City Council in the specialist housing department. Having introduced herself to us she asked, in light of us not being able to raise a deposit to purchase a home for Chris, if we would be interested in looking at a bungalow that was to be renovated and made available to her department. The idea was to split the large property into two and we could choose which half we would like for Chris and that it would be secured by a long-term tenancy.

Not what we really wanted but we had two questions that we quickly answered and made our minds up. Firstly, would we ever get the deposit to purchase and secondly how much longer did we want our son stuck in the hell hole he was in at present. Yes please! When can we see the property? It was only a week to wait and even more good news came when we were given the address. It was only three miles or ten minutes' drive from our home. What a difference to the journey we currently make twice a week that is over one hundred miles on each visit.

On arrival at the bungalow, we could see so much potential for Chris. It was so quiet, well until Chris gets tuned up and it would be his for as long as he wanted it. Our prayers had been answered.

Whilst the local authority would not budge on funding, although to this day we are still twisting their arm there was another shock looming. The company that the local authority, in particular, the case worker had favoured, informed them that they did not feel they could go ahead with caring for Chris and in any case would not be available to start at the bungalow for well over a year. What a result. The ICB had to come glove in hand and suggest we either look at other companies or we ask Kind Tailored Care if they would be able to look after Chris within the budget set by the authority.

WHOOPEE! At that meeting it gave me the greatest of pleasure to say to the senior lady representing the ICB, "NOW ITS YOU THAT HAS EGG ON YOUR FACE".

It then started to unravel how their case manager had been so deliberately awkward, how she had lied, how she showed her affinity to another company through a previous friendship, that being Tony in London. By this time, I had already made a formal complaint to the NHS who fund the largest proportion of Christopher's care. The document I sent in was around ten pages that showed how badly we and Kind Tailored care had been treated. It was in fact just a couple of days ago when Tina and I received the outcome of our complaint. A couple of apologies but much of their letter was trying to still blame us by using some facts that they had clearly trifled with to suit them. Altogether, not the result we wanted but we do not stop there. It has always been our intention to take the matter further and that is exactly what I intend to do. The next stop is the Governmental Ombudsman and if we are unsuccessful there then we will share our story with Fleet Street.

Oh, the one good thing that came out of this is that the Case manager that caused so much of the conflict has gone.

You will need to read on to discover who will be caring for Chris and how this has been attained.

CHAPTER 32

An Angel Without Wings

DO MIRACLES HAPPEN?

Many will say No! Some may sit on the fence, and some will accept that miracles may happen. I can say for sure that I have witnessed a miracle happening. Day after day, I have had the pleasure to witness an angel, one without wings, at work.

God knows how she achieves what she does in a day, where she gets all of her explosive energy. What she achieved with our son Chris, trust me, it was nothing short of amazing. God, I am sure, is the only one that knows where she gets all of her energy from.

There are other people that have formed bonds with Chris over the years but none like this little lady did in the eighteen months that she worked with our son. How did she manage to stop the regression that Chris was experiencing before Thornbury Nursing were appointed to look after our son? The answer is in fact simple. She treated Christopher with respect and taught him to respect her and others. I believe respect has another meaning you know and that is love. Chris grew to love this person, always wanting to know where she was if it was her day off.

I have said all of these things about this lady but not yet told you her name. She is very special not just to Chris but to us as well and we still stay in touch, even though she no longer looks after Chris. This lady's name is Nellie. An all so special lady that gave 110% each and every day to our son and gave him the care he required. When Nellie was looking after Chris on her own, well not quite and only with a carer from the home to support her, she had to work even harder. She said one day, "I may as well be on my own". On another occasion she said, "I never get time to sit down, I am on the go all day". Both statements were absolutely true. That was the only way she felt she was doing her best for our son.

Chris has a real fear of dogs and yet Nellie developed a very special way of moving Chris passed dogs when they turned up on the same patch. Thornbury took over after the abuse and neglect in November 2021 and Nellie soon got to grips with our son's personal care. His behaviours improved and the ripping of his clothes became almost something of the past.

Nelli has helped Chris achieve his strengths in so many ways. Let's look at cooking. Before Thornbury and Nelli arrived at the home it was absolute Taboo to use the beautiful kitchen in his flat. In fact, the management had removed the knobs off the cooker to prevent it being used. Their explanation for the removal was for safety, to stop the cooker being used dangerously. With that problem sorted, Nelli wasted no time at all in teaching Chris how to make various dishes including pancakes, pizzas from scratch, omelettes and curry.

On one particular day, having tried the meal by badgering one of the carers to share his lunch, Chris tried it, loved it and wanted to know how to cook it. It is actually called Jollof rice, looks like curry and must be pretty warming as it has several peppers and garlic within the ingredients. The next step of course was for Nelli and Chris to make this dish and to everyone's surprise Chris concentrated for two hours to complete the task. Just amazing what you can get someone to do if go about it the right way.

Nelli introduced walking as a great way to fend off bad behaviours. I don't mean a little stroll around outside, Nelli's idea of a walk was around ten thousand steps. In fact, in two days, when Chris was having a difficult time, he and his wonder carer actually walked twenty-six thousand steps. Chris returned to the home still looking fit but without any signs of a bad behaviour.

Continuing the theme of walking, just before Nelli and her team were withdrawn she teamed up with Chris for a month's walking for autism. They each achieved over half a million steps and raised lots of money for Walk for Autism.

Swimming, another favourite of our son and Nelli saw to it that he went to the local pool almost every Monday morning. It wasn't proper swimming, but Chris loved it. In fact, with the ingenuity of Nelli things got better. She encouraged Chris to wear armbands and they helped him so much, mostly still just splashing around but by the noises he would make it was obvious he was enjoying himself.

Another positive interaction was drawing, especially when the weather conditions were poor. Until Nelli arrived Chris spent so much of his time just sitting around, doing nothing positive and his carers doing little to change the situation. They would also just sit around typing on a tablet, supposedly making notes. They made hardly any effort to interact with a young man that was crying out for positive things to take up his time. Nellie changed things for the better. When dogs were anywhere near on a walk there would be lots of hugs and reassurance that Chris was safe and that the dogs would not hurt him.

Nelli also taught Chris the art of Square Breathing and that has indeed come to his rescue so many times.

Before telling you about the positives that Nelli introduced, I was talking about the tearing of clothes and shoes, and I can tell you that the cost of replacing those items more than halved in the first few weeks our angel was onboard. Christopher again looked very tidy, and his hair was cared for properly, with no sign of matting that had been so prominent. That, put in simple terms, was because if Christopher said, "No Hairbrush", the staff at the home would not bother. Nelli on the other hand, would not take no for an answer. She would give Chris the time he needed to process the request and then he would allow her to groom his hair properly.

What is amazing to us it that the local authority failed to recognise how after the incidents of November 2021, and the introduction of Thornbury Nursing how quickly Christopher's behaviours improved. Move on to early in 2023 when Thornbury Nurses were removed and again the local authority have failed to see how quickly our son has again regressed. Is it not obvious to these people in authority to recognise the stark difference between properly trained carers and those that are brought in from agencies, not having had any proper training at all. To care for anyone on the autistic spectrum you need to have an understanding of autism, a true and in depth understanding. I cannot bring to mind one person working at our son's care home at the moment that has any understanding of autism whatsoever. As Nellie once said to us, that she believes she is caring for Chris virtually single handed at the home, but if that is what's needed, she will continue to do so. Oh Nellie, how Chris and us, his parents miss you.

The ICB and the Local Authority are clearly guilty in more ways than one but mostly by not admitting that Christopher does have very Complex needs and therefore a need for specialist carers. There are two reasons for them not accepting our son's needs. The first reason was because none of those people making the decisions about this complex young man hardly ever visited him and when they did the visit lasted little over five minutes. That is not a guess, it is fact, and we have proof. They, the ICB and the social worker at that time must have been highly trained in autism and special needs to be able to make their conclusions in such a short time.

It must also be pointed out that the seniors at the ICB and local authority, would not listen to professionals that were adamant that Chris was very complex and needed and still today needs specialist care to match his complexity. Here lies the second reason I believe they will not accept they have made errors with Chris's care package. That they will not put their hands into the City's coffers and pay that little extra that could make so much difference.

I can assure all of my readers that this matter is not closed, and we shall continue to fight for what Christopher so rightly deserves.

Nelli, Chris cannot wait for you to visit him in his bungalow, just as soon as he moves in. He will be baking you a Lemon Drizzle cake to have with a very special cup of Tea.

God bless you Nellie and thank you for everything you have done for our son.

CHAPTER 33

What Real Care Looks Like

I bet by now many of you have guessed who will be caring for Christopher in his new home, his bungalow that is so close to his Mummy and Daddy and of course his brother Charlie.

Any company, whether it be a Tailor, a Farmer, a Food Store or perhaps even a Furniture manufacturer can only ever become as good as the person at the top. The person that writes the script if you like or the person drawing the blueprint. If the person at the top stops caring about those they supply or those that help to provide the service, in other words, their employees, then that company is batting on a dodgy wicket. Sometimes the demise of a company occurs because the person at the top, the CEO gets bored, gets fed up or perhaps even gets too greedy or they stop working their business themselves.

So, the sign of a good company and what it might achieve no matter how new it might be, can be seen by studying the person or persons at the top. I firmly believe this is the case whether a company has millions of staff, or maybe is made up of just the right number to complete the task in hand, with an eye on growing at the right time and the right speed and with a leader that always has an eye on the business, its future and the employees that make it all possible.

Why do I write this sort of thing in a book like this? Well, this is what I personally looked for when hunting for a care company to look after our son, our treasure. I wanted nothing but the best and I now believe with my hand on heart that my wife and I have achieved the best for Christopher.

I mentioned how a leader must be someone special, someone who cares, and I know the lady that formed Kind Tailored Care has those attributes in abundance.

Sophie, with thirty years' experience in the care industry is the CEO of a care company that has everything built into its name. KIND – Always prepared to listen, to go beyond the normal. TAILORED – To ensure that the care given is especially designed to keep your child, your family member safe and always as happy as can be. CARE – The dictionary says about care that it is what is necessary for the health, welfare, maintenance and protection of someone or something. Having spent many hours with Sophie and her management team I am confident these are all attributes bred and expected within Kind Tailored Care.

I believe staff should feel really good about themselves if they are accepted into the team because without doubt, they are put through the most rigorous training before being accepted. Mind, perhaps a warning might be that the same staff should always treat those they are caring for with the right mindset, lest they wish to see another side of their boss. Sophie, and rightly so, will not have the credibility of her wonderful company compromised. The old saying "The Customer is always right" is one I believe Sophie and her team believe in. The right attitude is so important in the care industry and whilst Kind Tailored Care are still new to us and our son, from what we have seen thus far it is wonderful.

Laura, the lady appointed as Christopher's Care Manager at the bungalow is so highly qualified and so understanding. Together with another lady, named Lisa they have started the transition with Chris from his home of five years to his new home back at his bungalow. The regression we had witnessed since Thornbury Nursing were withdrawn from the home in February 2023 has already started to hide its ugly head. How has this happened so quickly, you might ask. The answer is quite simple. The staff now working with Chris from Kind Tailored Care have been trained to a very high standard and are constantly interacting with him, keeping him busy and not allowing boredom to turn into unnecessary bad behaviours. It is just such a shame that the ICB and Local Authority in Southampton would not provide further funding for our son's transition, meaning the KTC staff are only at Chris's current home for three days each week.

However, these same staff will be tasked to teach and train all new recruits to that same high standard at Kind Tailored Care, ensuring that Christopher's future is bright. Very Bright Indeed.

Having a backbone to your business, someone that can look after all the day-to-day running is also so important and at Kind Tailored Care another very special lady named Loren sees to it that everything runs smoothly. It is just an amazing team and one that I would recommend in an instant.

So, what else have Kind tailored Care, in particular Sophie, done to ensure it is their company that does indeed care for Chris. One of the answers and it may feel strange is because Chris is so lovable. Every one that encounters time with our son is drawn in by his loving nature and beautiful looks and, so I am told by the care team, that they recognise the love and hard work that his parents are always prepared to give to win so many battles on his behalf. That is why Sophie has chosen to offer the same standard of care to Christopher, that she would have, had the authorities agreed with those that gave their professional advice that has so sadly been ignored.

Look at it all this way. On this occasion, it was Chris that was in the shop window. An irresistible young man that so deserves recompense for so much of his care and I am absolutely certain that he will receive nothing but the best from the company we have chosen. Finally, I so believe that something vitally important to anyone, is to have that feeling of being a part of something special, family life, if you like. We are, in my opinion, a wonderful loving family. Here for each other, to love and support and I now believe our family has grown. In my opinion a family does not necessarily have to be a group of blood relatives, but it does have to be a group of human beings that care for each other. We have invited into our family people like Sophie, Laura, Lisa and Loren, all because they want to care for one of our own and in this instance, I also believe they have not put their financial gain first. Yes, of course they need to be paid, to earn a living, life would be difficult without that, but I am without doubt sure that these ladies have put a young man's future, before any financial gain. We have even had carers from Kind Tailored Care that have been working on the transition to his bungalow, met Chris just one or two times and have asked to work with him permanently. These ladies, Kaddie and Dawn, to name but two, have recognised right away how special Christopher is, almost inviting them to be part of his life. Just like Nellie, the "special one" from Thornbury Nursing, Sophie and her team would it seems do anything for our very special young man and we thank you all for that.

CHAPTER 34

He's Coming Home!

When Christopher's time came to an end at one of the best specialist schools, in our opinion, in the country, that is Hill House, in the heart of the New Forest, we had a really difficult task on our hands. That task was to find an adult placement that would be as good as Hill House with staff that could equal those our son had become accustomed to for the previous five years.

You have already heard that after visiting eleven residential homes we had to make a decision and thinking we had had made the right one, applied for a place at a home in the north of the county. It was sort of all right for the first couple of years but guess what?

WE GOT IT WRONG! After two to three years and a change in management the establishment started to go downhill, causing so many problems for our son and no doubt, having spoken to another parent whose son is at the same home problems for some of the other residents. Without doubt the deterioration at the home was accelerated in November 2021, when as I told you earlier Chris was abused and neglected. Just to remind you, it was at that time that the home neglected to give our son his anti-psychotic medication for twenty two days, failed to call in a doctor or seek any medical advice following a serious injury to Chris's arm and to top it all thirteen bruises were found on his body when the case manager of that time and parents demanded that body maps be completed. None of those bruises have ever been explained.

I mean, how can you possibly trust anyone or any organisation after that? Particularly as those responsible still remain working in the home as if nothing has happened. As I also mentioned earlier, a legal case is ongoing, so I dare not say too much more on the subject.

However, this chapter apart from those first few paragraphs is to be Happy! Why? 'Cause he's coming home! Yes, that's right Chris is coming home, well at least back to Southampton and within three miles of where we live.

It means that we will not have those twice weekly journeys of over one hundred miles each to visit him. It means that we can see Chris virtually every day of the week as he can us. It means he will have staff that truly care about him, that he can choose when and where he wants to go out, what he wants to eat and to do anything else that takes his fancy.

The staff we have chosen can work to rebuild Christopher's confidence in himself, to put a halt to the regression that has happened since Thornbury Nurses were withdrawn and to ensure that our son enjoys his life to the full. Boy, does he deserve that!

It has taken one year and nine months to find Chris his new home and having been through so much to achieve what we have has put us under so much stress and strain. Has it been worth it? Of course it has. As a parent, if you love your son or daughter, you instinctively do whatever it takes to achieve and give them the best. If you are not prepared to do that then I think as a parent, you must question yourself.

Ultimately, Chris will enjoy a quality of life that many of us, sometimes take for granted. Chris will be able to meet with his siblings, his nieces, nephews and others he probably still remembers from times gone by. You must remember, save for brief visits back home, an hour or two at a time, he has not spent any meaningful time with most of his family.

Most importantly, for us it will mean, with much of the problems dealt with, that we can become Christopher's Mum and Dad again.

Three weeks ago, transition started for Chris with the introduction of some of his new carers, experienced, without doubt caring and with an empathetic attitude, quickly attempting to halt the regression and prepare Chris for this long-awaited move.

Something else that our son is enjoying is the delivery of his brand new motability vehicle. We had to be very careful this time around with our choice, that he had enough head room. In his previous car his head was touching the roof but in this one, he calls it his Minibus, he has enough head room and space around him.

We always used to say on a drive out that we would have to stop and give the car a drink but with this one, being fully electric I have not found the equivalent words. That's not really a problem as we don't ever charge the car whilst Chris is in it and when he gets to his bungalow, he will have his very own home charging unit. It is so lovely to drive, it's a Citroen Berlingo built especially with seven seats, as Chris must sit at the very back for the safety of the driver. You won't see many of those on the road but look out if you do see one, if it's a beautiful royal blue then it could be our Chris on board. I must thank Reg the guy at Wilmoth's that has looked after us so well.

For months, since Thornbury were withdrawn Chris has only been able to go for a drive if we were visiting or if the home happens to have a driver around. But here's the thing, they refused to drive his BMW saying it was too posh and that we had put too many rules in place and now they won't drive Blossom, sorry that's the name given by us for the Berlingo. Chris loves nothing more to go for a drive in the country, listening to Heart 80's music and the volume set at number twelve.

Now, with the transition started Kind Tailored Care staff are more than happy to take Chris out as much as he wants them to. Stop somewhere nice, where hopefully too many dogs are not around and let Chris spend as long as he likes, just walking.

Once he gets home to the bungalow, he will be given help to plan his meals, decide what he wants to do and where he wants to go each and every day. Even if he decides not to go out, that will not be a problem as his bungalow is located in such a quiet and peaceful area, just a few minutes away from beautiful countryside. It is just half an hour's drive from the New Forest and about the same if he wants to go to the Coffee Cup. By the way, The Coffee Cup, that's a large café on the sea front at Southsea where Chris used to visit quite regularly and where he enjoyed fish and chips on the beach. That for sure, I think will be number one on his list of places to revisit.

Chris will have a book full of pictures of places he used to love to visit making choosing very easy for him. A similar book full of meals that we know our son likes will be made ready for him, so that it is he that chooses what he eats from now on, not having food pushed upon him that looks boring, dry or uninviting Incidentally it will be Chris that is encouraged to cook his meals, not to be waited upon. We want Chris to learn to be as independent as possible.

This homecoming is the start of a new beginning. We will never know just how much Christopher has been affected by his time in that residential home but what we can do is be there for him, helping to make sure his future is rosy.

WELCOME HOME MY BOY!

Charles Parker

CHAPTER 35

A Word From Mum

Without doubt, it would be wrong of me to bring this journey of an amazing young man without giving space to the most important person in Christopher's life to express how she has felt, how she feels now and what she holds in her thoughts for the future.

Tina, a wonderful wife and a mother that is topped by no one in the world. Her love for us all has always been there in abundance, her will to fight alongside me for the benefit of our family never questioned. I now want Tina, a very special lady, a very special mother, to bring her thoughts to you and as she shares those thoughts spare a thought what she has given up at times to ensure that our family has also enjoyed the best that she had to offer.

So, it's all yours Tina, please share your thoughts with us all.

Hi everyone,

At the beginning it was a dark place. Moments that I remember being told that Chris was not meeting his milestones and was delayed and suggestions of autism. I remember the road we were travelling, and I was left devastated when it was confirmed that Chris was on the spectrum. However after a day of self-pity I picked myself up and realised that I needed to step up and learn how to become my son's voice and one of his advocates. I did this despite having challenges with my own confidence.

I guess that information and learning can be likened to the old saying "for warned is forearmed. You need to know something about what you are facing to make you stronger and better prepared. So, I looked through the internet and came across an article about a lady who needed to lock all her doors and windows to keep her child safe and stop her rooms not being destroyed. I never for one moment thought this might be the same for Chris but it gave me an insight in some things like home safety that could be important for the future, and some of them most certainly were!

It was a big adjustment to our lives when we accepted Chris's autism, we all grieved. Some relatives brushing it off and saying it was something he would grow out of, but not me. I knew something for sure; the good and the bad would make us all stronger and that we would learn to cope. Some people would say to us how do you do it and you simply reply I didn't realise I had a choice; I just do what I have to.

I Believe that Chris has made us better people, I have a newfound respect for those living and caring for people with disabilities, never ignoring them and making me engage with them, showing them human kindness whenever I can. I Truly believe it has made me a better person; I am thankful for that.

Christopher is an incredible person; I see the potential in him although I never look to compare or measure him against others. We are all on a unique journey and it's beautiful to be travelling it with him.

They say it takes a village to raise a child, and that is especially true when you have a person with additional needs; if you are reading this and are at the start of your journey, then my best advice is never to be scared to ask for help, it does not make you weak or inadequate as a person but has the potential to make you much stronger. Throughout Chris's life we have had some incredible people that have been friends to us and to Christopher and who have helped and supported us as a family.

In the beginning there was so little support, but virtual groups became a lifeline and a virtual hug meant so much. Talking to others became like therapy and still is the best way to share and give and receive advice to help you to move forward.

One the next page I want to share a poem with you, it came to me just the other day, hearing how many people view persons with any mental health condition or indeed disabilities, sometimes as less than. This was so true for Christopher who with his behaviours that challenge you, could see that people were afraid, not realising that all behaviours are communications; we just need to understand and learn more.

This just makes me what to be an advocate more for those especially who cannot find the words themselves. We are all the same, unique only in our challenges but all humans.

I Am Human

I am human, I am just like you.
I am loved by family and friends,
When you see me know that I am like you.

Yes, I may have more challenges.
But these are not mine to change.
But for you to understand.
Understand my world and yours will be better.

I am untouched by the ugliness of actions and others' thoughts,
So my world is a happier place,
Join me and understand!
You will see I am human just like you.

Yes, I have a label, but it does not define me,
I am me first, a person who is living,
Loving, learning and growing just like you.

I am an individual and unique in my talents.
I may need extra support.
But I can achieve the same, just like you.

Autism is a rainbow of colours,
And special people that enrich our lives
Step inside, find out, learn more,
Find out that we are not a condition!

We are not to be feared or ignored,
We are amazing as is every human on this planet.
I am human and I matter too.

By Tina Parker

CHAPTER 36

What Does the Future Hold?

Good Question! Some might argue that we can do nothing about the future, but I beg to differ.

For those of you out there that have a child or maybe more than one that has Autism, or additional needs, I truly believe that you must think very carefully before answering the question that forms the title of this chapter.

When it comes to our autistic children, do we take the attitude, like the very old song "like I mentioned earlier" by Doris Day when she portrayed the words "What Will Be, Will Be, Que Sera Sera. Within the song Doris Day also sings, "The future's not ours to see", a very true statement but with help I again believe anyone can, with the right support make a significant difference to what they have left of their lives or can have a significant influence on the lives of those they care for.

So please just think, do you as a parent or maybe a sibling undertake to do all you can to change and improve the future of your loved one or are you one just to treat the future for your child, brother or sister with an air of "Oh well never mind", it is what it is.

Having recently watched a programme on the BBC, narrated and produced by Chris Packham, who is on the Autistic Spectrum himself it has made me think, Can I do more for my children? Can Tina and I do more for others on the spectrum? The programme was about three young adults, all on the spectrum and how they were dealing with the issues that make life difficult for them and what they, with some help, have done about it.

Before I tell you more about one of those young persons in particular, let me just tell those that have never heard of Chris Packham what he has achieved and how successful he has made his life so far.

Chris was brought up in Southampton and grew up with a natural love of animals and nature as a whole. As a young man and after university he found himself working on the CBBC nature series, The Really Wild Show, where he was very successful. Since then, Chris has been on many other television programmes, most if my memory serves me well, about nature and everyone so interesting. In short, an amazing man. I do not want to tempt fate but feel pretty sure you will all know David Attenborough. I for one and no doubt many others have thought, "Who will take this amazing man's place on our screens?" The world will never be the same without Sir David and we all fear the day, but I am convinced that Christopher Packham could be someone who could grow into Sir David's shoes.

When I wrote my first book, "Tell It as it Is" in 2007 I had the good fortune to serve Christopher's parents who had become customers of ours. They too, were wonderful people and whenever my wife and I delivered their orders they loved to ask about our boys, wanting to know about their progress. Of course, they also loved to talk about their son Chris and to tell us about some of his childhood ventures and show us some of the birds and animals that had died naturally, and that Chris had got preserved. Having spent all of my early years in what was a small country village on the edge of Southampton, it was just such a joy to see the treasures that young master Packham had around his parents' home.

It was also wonderful, having written my first book, when I received a very long, detailed letter from Chris, thanking me and encouraging me to write more. I am sorry Mr Packham that it has taken so long to put pen to paper again. Perhaps, I could use the excuse that I had spent so much of my spare time watching Chris on his TV ventures.

Back now to the brilliant programme that Chris brought to our screens about autism. There was a young lad on there that was what most of us call nonverbal, in other words cannot talk. But yes, he can! He talks through an especially adapted laptop. Listening to that young man truly opened my eyes and my mind that there was for sure more out there for my severely autistic son and hope for many more parents throughout our world.

The Autistic spectrum is of course massive, many on it as different as chalk and cheese. For instance, I do not think my son is anywhere near the same as the three that appeared on the TV programme but like the nonverbal lad, I do believe our son has much more to offer than he has done so far, especially when he again has a consistency of good carers.

The example the lad on the TV gave was about him moving on from Tellie

Tubbies that he had loved from a baby, right through to his teens. He has truly done that and not only has he surprised his parents and family, but they also feel very proud. Perhaps most important of all is that he has proved to the world what can be achieved given the correct encouragement.

The programme, shown over two weeks concluded by each of the three young adults producing a short film that could be watched first by their families and then exposed to all on the television. It basically covered what many with ASD do, that is known as masking. Putting on an act because they need to fit in. On each of the three short films they were able to show their family members what they are really like. By the end of this brilliant programme the masks were down, and we were able to see these three people as they really are. Each of them feeling better about themselves and proving that they really didn't need to rely on the mask.

Both my wife and I learnt so much. What we didn't know is how many people with autism mask their problems because they feel ashamed of how they portray to others. They want to fit in with others. Some with jobs, in particular hide their real identity. The programme showed there is no shame in being autistic and that so many more can do away with their masking and just be themselves.

From where Christopher was at his last school, doing so well, having gone there still on "P" levels for all subjects and then moving on to level 2 on the National Curriculum for all subjects, I truly believe he can achieve more. That is providing we can put a halt to the regression he has shown since the Master of Care, Thornbury Nurses, were removed from his residential home and he was again placed in the care of those that had neglected and abused him.

Once Chris is established in his own bungalow with carers from Kind Tailored Care that are competent, I think it possible that our son may have a few surprises up his sleeve for us. My wife and I want to get him back into college, maybe doing more of his bricklaying, perhaps learning more about farming, we are not sure, but we will search for opportunities.

What we are sure of is that we shall be working hard to give him the chances he needs to make more of his life. Physically he is very fit. If we can help him control his behaviours and he does not have to use bad behaviours to tell us something is wrong or maybe what he wants, then we believe he has a good chance to make some fantastic progress.

One of the things we are going to work on is using his laptop or his I pad to ask his questions and to tell us his needs. The fact that Chris has been able to read and spell extremely well from around five years old gives us hope.

The search is on now to find someone, perhaps a speech and language therapist to help Chris and make his future so much brighter.

It is wonderful to finally think that we have found the right carers to look after Christopher properly, with the right attitude. To ensure that no matter what comes in the future for Christopher that he will be kept safe, that he will remain happy in his bungalow and will know that we, his parents will always do whatever we can for him.

I suppose the thoughts of Tina and me must now turn to being able to become parents once more and not always having to engulf ourselves in battles galore. To share a certain peace with our sons and of course everyone else that forms part of our family.

Rest assured though, if the need arises to do battle once more, we most certainly will be ready. With what has gone on in the past it is very difficult to lead a life that is not always on hight alert.

I mentioned earlier in this chapter that Tina and I want to help others either on the spectrum or those caring for them and I now want to share something that is quite exciting and that will, I am sure, help so many.

Earlier in the book I mentioned that Tina and I have our own online business teaching others to know how they can use 100% pure essential oils and purchase them if they wish. We have team members from many countries and have recently started to give online presentations to them showing how we use our oils to help our sons and others on the ASD Spectrum with their behaviours. We want to help as many as possible, but also want to build our business back up to where it was before it was knocked back when we put our son and his problems at the care home first.

One of the ladies that recently answered our advert on Facebook and attended a presentation, discovered during our chats that our main ambition in life is to help others. She has invited my wife and I to meet at her farm, where she has converted a massive barn into something where talks, workshops and communal get togethers can be held.

This opportunity was not to be missed, but I had to tell Megan, I had already been talking to Simon, the guy who I mentioned earlier, that had helped Christopher so much. Simon also wanted Tina and I to team up with him and build something special; workshops and talks that could help so many and introduce them to my books.

Our dear friend Simon who helped with Chris at a very difficult time in 2015, is keen to join me, my wife Tina and Megan by combining our passion to help others.

Now, as soon as I mentioned this to Megan, who incidentally is an experienced Innate Health Psychologist, she immediately came up with the idea that we should all work together and that is exactly what we are planning. We are already working very hard to bring our mission to life. To help as many as possible on the spectrum, those that are carers and also those professionals that perhaps want to learn more, so that they can make more informed decisions as they go about their work. Giving them the opportunity to learn from those that have the experience of living with autism, like Tina and I with over twenty years' experience. Add to that the amazing knowledge and professionalism that Simon, Megan and Howard, that's Megan's husband will have to offer and without doubt we will make a difference.

Megan, incidentally, has seven children, some of them now adult and three of them on the spectrum and one more that is in the middle of a diagnosis.

We have a joint mission and working together as a great team, uniting the skills we each have, believe we can achieve so much and help so many. By pulling together we can turn our individual dreams into reality.

OUR COLLECTIVE MISSION - Taking people from the same world, the world of autism, and teaching them to talk the talk. We will not assume; we shall listen and give everyone a voice!

Megan and her husband have created a space where everyone is welcome and with our joint help can become stronger. Megan also feels that living with a child or children on the spectrum is not easy. Like us she has many years of experience. Gaining the experience is not easy, it has to be worked at and some find that hard. With a spectrum that is so long and so complex that is totally understandable.

Simon, with thirty years of health care experience has his own company, is always available to listen and offer advice and will. I am sure, be the anchor that our mission needs to ensure its success.

You will be able to find out more about each of us and about our mission at our group on Facebook. Tell It As It Is - Charles Parker or by using this link. https://www.facebook.com/groups/111759617555183 Join now, and follow our journey, keep up to date with our mission and find out more about the amazing people that are supporting Tina and me. In the group you will find out more about Simon and Megan and how you can contact them.

I do hope this chapter has not just been of interest but a real help if you have anyone with autism within your family or if you have friends that are in the same boat as we are. Perhaps the most important thing for any person on the spectrum to experience is true happiness, no matter what they choose to do in their life or are encouraged to do just be happy within their parameters. You know, I think that last sentence could be taken on board by us all, no matter who we are, what problems we have, try our best to be happy and enjoy whatever we take on in our lives.

In conclusion I want to share a poem that I wrote and included in my first book. Having written hundreds of poems in the past I thought it would be easy to write a new one for this book. Try as I may, I find myself stuck. Quite recently when discussing the problem with a friend he said something to me that put my mind at rest. "Charles, he said, there is nothing more you can do or say that would improve that poem in your first book. It says everything, please, don't try to mend what is not broken."

So, I have taken my friends advise and conclude my work with the same poem as I did in 2007. Please read and enjoy.

Thank you for reading this true story, one that has brought many tears to my eyes and also brought so many smiles as I transformed my memories onto paper.

Much strength and love to you all from our family and big hugs from Chris.

A Poem For Autism

Our son is autistic, so what the hell!
You look at him most times, you never could tell.
There may be tantrum, some screams at his Bruv
But then there's the cuddle that shows us his love

Why should we worry, we can't change him now
We must press on forward, the question is how.
I'll tell you the secret; we'll hold our heads high.
For we're stuck with this problem till the day that we die

We'll let no one torment us, give us a bad time.
Very few understand, far less give a dime.
We'll make sure we tell them, yes announce full of pride.
Our son is autistic, we have nothing to hide.

We call on all parents with kids just like Chris.
To help raise awareness of problems like his
They all deserve more so don't miss a chance.
Shout LOUD, shout OFTEN, Their lives to Enhance.

Written by Charles Parker, the author of
TELL IT AS IT IS and TELL IT AS IT IS THE SEQUEL

And dedicated to his son Christopher and Autistic People everywhere.

Charles Parker